Dear Shah Rukh:

In Your Shadows, I Found My Light

A Memoir of Hope, Healing, and the Man Who Inspired It All

PRIYANKA SRIVASTAVA

Clever Fox®
PUBLISHING

CLEVER FOX PUBLISHING
Chennai, India

Published by CLEVER FOX PUBLISHING 2025

ISBN: 978-93-6707-710-8

Disclaimer:
This is a personal memoir. It is not affiliated with, nor endorsed by Shah Rukh Khan or his representatives.

Contents

Contents

First Love

First love stories are so compelling and, like many *Firsts*, first love, too, is the most memorable experience everyone goes through only once in their lifetime. It is always special and unforgettable. The impression it leaves on the heart lasts for a lifetime. It is pure and innocent. There is no love like the first love. No matter what stage of life we are in, our first love moves us in an inherently unique way. It introduces us to feelings we have never had before, for better or for worse, and is accompanied by a sense of wonder, intrigue, and excitement.

We will find several stories around these two words. Different people have described their first love in different ways. For some, it was love at first sight, while for others, it was one-sided love. Some have an eternal love story. For others, it was a painful ending. For some, it brought a feeling of ecstasy, while many others felt a sense of devastation. Everyone has a different first love experience, but the essence of it is the same.

Falling in love is an incomparable feeling. The first time we feel a spark, it is indescribable. The imprint it leaves on our hearts and brains stays with us for the rest of our lives. Every first associated with the first love is something our heart wants to hold on to forever: the first eye lock, the first smile, the first touch—something we vividly remember yet seldom talk about with others.

My First Love experience is deeply personal and exclusive. At eight, when I was somewhere between a toddler and a teenager, or what they call a 'tween', I lived in my dreamland. I did not even know the meaning of love. Attraction was an unknown concept to me. The only thing I was attracted to was my little Barbie. The only thing I loved was the Chocolate Bar ice cream. I was young enough to fall for anyone, yet I did.

I first saw him thirty years ago, riding a bike, singing joyfully. He was young and charming. He was of average height and was brown. His eyes were deep and expressive. A naughty, devil-like smile flashed on his face. The black jeans and the tan-coloured leather jacket over a white T-shirt made him even more attractive. His carefree and friendly attitude was captivating. As he rode his bike, the wind did some kind of magic to his black bear-like hair. As his hair swayed with the wind, so did my heart.

I fell in love instantly. It felt warm and happy. Butterflies fluttered and swirled through my stomach. At that very moment, I was convinced that I was in love, for the very first time. It was at that moment I understood what it feels like when someone says, 'My heart skipped a beat'. The world seemed new. It was more beautiful. I still remember how I could not stop smiling, lost in his thoughts. I would feel shy and giggly thinking about him. Every time I saw him; my heart would melt away. I was smitten beyond my imagination.

It has been three decades, but this feeling is still the same. This is the only constant in my always-changing life. He is married and so am I. He has three kids, and I have one. His love for his wife runs deep, while my love for my husband is intense. He is in one part of the country, and I am in another. He is in a different profession, and I am in a different one. But none of these factors have made any difference in the way I feel about him. My love for him is pure, eternal, selfless, and unconditional. I loved him when I saw him first and I love him today and I will love him till my last breath. Even to this date, my heart begins to race with a blushing face. I hear bells ringing in my head and can feel the warmth of my blood running through my veins at the mere mention of his name.

I know I may never get a chance to express my feelings to him in person, hence, this book. This is an attempt to convey my feelings to the first love of my life. Through the series of letters, I wanted to share a part of myself with the one I have loved my entire life. As we move from one letter to another, we embark on a journey through time, emotions, and the miracles he has woven into my life unknowingly.

Each letter speaks of the impact he has had on me, as I share my firsthand experiences, recollections, and reflections. Just like the first love, there are many other firsts associated with him, and I want to relive them with these letters.

From the small town of Varanasi to the bustling streets of Mumbai and Chennai, and from the fast-paced rhythm of daily life to the quiet moments of self-discovery, these letters are a celebration of love, resilience, and the enduring connection between me and him. As we journey through these pages, you will witness how a love so pure can shape a lifetime of emotions. Each letter is not just a memory, it is a living reminder of admiration, the beauty of dreams, and the unshaken faith in the power of love.

With each letter in the book, I pray a little harder that I can get the message across to the one it is intended for. However, whether or not he ever reads these words, this is my way of expressing a love that has stood the test of time. Let us begin.

From *#Deewana* to *#Jawan*, *#loveyouhamesha* my dear Shah Rukh Khan ♥.

Hey There - It's Me!!!

Dear Shah Rukh,

As someone who has followed your journey for years... Oh, wait, do I sound like a stalker? Before you think I am, let me clarify - I am just a... Okay, let us find out who I am.

Allow me to introduce myself. Officially, I am known as Priyanka, but my loved ones call me Varsha, Rain, or Pree. You can call me anything–just call me. I will share my number!

I've been handling corporate chaos for the last sixteen years—and I must say, I'm getting better at it day by day. I'm an expert at manipulating my husband into doing things my way; while letting him believe it was all his brilliant idea.

Juggling a two-year-old daughter who thinks sleep is optional and a five-year-old pup who believes shoes are chewing toys is child's play for me. A loving daughter and a dutiful daughter-in-law, I'm also the eldest sibling to the two strangest (but most adorable) creatures on Earth.

An IT professional by day and a writer at heart, I'm also the kind of friend people tend to keep forever—or maybe I just don't let go off anyone that easily. From a bird's-eye view, everything looks picture-perfect. But take a closer look, and you'll see my life is a full-blown circus—and I'm the ringmaster, whip in hand and smile on face. And through it all, your films, your interviews, and your words have often been the soundtrack playing in the background, sometimes keeping me sane, sometimes reminding me to dream bigger.

I grew up watching you, arguing with everyone over you, fighting my siblings for you, and breaking countless rules for you. When adversity struck, you were my North Star. You, Shah Rukh, are my caffeine in human form, keeping me awake and inspired. You have been a source of inspiration, a reason to fall in love, a beacon of hope, and a symbol of resilience, shaping countless moments in my journey. Amidst the pandemonium, I am a tini-mini admirer in your vast sea of fans. Not a day passes without thoughts of you crossing my mind.

Why am I sharing this with you? Well, who else but you, Shah Rukh? You have been more than just a Bollywood star; you have been my cheerleader in this chaotic game of life. From my awkward crush phase where I adorned my notebook with your pictures, much to my parents' dismay, to navigating the difficulties of adulthood, you have been there.

Your movies have been my Friday night therapy sessions, your interviews, my dose of wisdom, and sometimes mischief, and your iconic poses—let us just say I have attempted a few in front of the mirror, often with disastrous results. Why is it that you and only YOU look good in those tilted postures with your arms spread?

From bustling parties with friends to quiet and lonely evenings curled up with your films, you have been a constant companion. In the hardships of my career and in the tranquility of my marriage, you have been with me through it all. It is only fair that you get a glimpse into the life of someone whose days have been brightened by your charisma and charm. After all, you have touched my life in more than a thousand ways.

So, why write to you? Well, Shah Rukh, I have tried almost everything to reach you! My Twitter feed practically turns into a shrine to you during #AskSRK sessions, filled with tweets in hopes of catching your eye. Unfortunately, luck has not been on my side. I have never received a response. But I have not given up. I have thought of some creative ways to get in touch. I have tried sweet-talking your guards outside 'Mannat', tried to get to you through some fan clubs, considered pretending to be a journalist, though my journalism skills are about as polished as a cardboard cutout, and even toyed with the idea of getting a job at Mumbai airport just to run into you. And yes, I will admit, I once entertained the crazy idea of skydiving in your backyard. Silly, right? Yes, that is what I am.

Although my attempts may seem crazy, they stem from a genuine desire to connect with someone who has profoundly influenced my life. However, it seems quite impossible to get to you, Shah Rukh.

Amidst all these wild ideas, my husband's WhatsApp status, 'Keep it simple, silly', finally made sense. So, here I am, choosing the old-school way with this letter. It is a humble attempt to reach out directly, hoping my message finds its way to you. Maybe, in the midst of all the fanfare and everyday chaos, this straightforward approach will resonate. Hoping it does.

You might be wondering, Shah Rukh, why now? Well, it is already late. Isn't it? Procrastination is not good. It has already been three decades since I have kept these feelings to myself. I think it is high time to act upon it. Afterall, you have always been present in my thoughts and dreams.

Speaking of dreams, lately, I find myself dreaming of you more often. These are some whimsical dreams. In one, I swooped in and saved you from a mob of rowdy girls. Yes! I know! In real-time, you would not want to be saved, that too from girls, but it was my dream, and I was the hero! In another one, I found us dancing on a cloud, with you twirling me around like you do with your actresses. Another time, we were solving mysteries together, Sherlock Holmes style, and you complimented me on my detective skills. And then there was the dream where we travelled the world in a hot-air balloon, exploring exotic lands and laughing like old friends. And let us not forget the dream where you taught me how to perform your *'Chaiyan Chaiyan'* dance moves, and I nailed them! Sometimes you are the next-door neighbor and other times a stranger at a nightclub asking me out.

I am sure a few more dreams, I will end up replacing your bodyguards or starring as your leading lady in your next movie. Yes! Insane dreams.

When I wake up, I cannot help but wish I had not. Thoughts of these dreams stick with me throughout the day, blurring the lines between what is real and what is in my imagination. Each dream leaves me yearning for more.

I have already lost my heart to you, Shah Rukh; and now, I fear I might be losing my mind too. So, reaching out to you feels like a necessary step to maintain some semblance of sanity. I want you to know how much you mean to me, how important and adorable you are to me.

As I pen these words, I realize there is nothing new I can say that has not been said before. You must have heard everything I said, or I am going to say more than a million times, but what do I do? I don't know how to say the same thing in different ways, so I will keep it simple: I love you, Shah Rukh. You are the first love of my life. Okay, I will be honest, you are the second love of my life, the first being my dad!

Jokes aside, Shah Rukh, my affection for you goes far beyond mere fandom; it is a deep admiration for the person behind the actor. Your talent and charisma are incredible, but what truly captivates me is your kindness, intelligence, and humility. You inspire me not just with your performances on screen but with your charm and wisdom off the screen.

In many ways, you remind me of a bright star guiding me in the right direction, a beacon that lights up my path even in the darkest times. When I watch your interviews or read about your journey, I see a person who has faced challenges with resilience and came out stronger. That is what I admire the most about you—your ability to remain humble and grounded, despite your immense success.

Words often fall short in capturing the depth of my feelings, but to put it simply: just as Shri Krishna was for Meera, you are for me—a divine presence that permeates every aspect of my being. Your influence reaches far beyond your movies; it touches my heart and soul. You have been a source of inspiration, comfort, and joy, and I am immensely grateful for the impact you've had on my life.

So, I wanted to take this opportunity to express my love and admiration for you, not just as an actor, but as an extraordinary human being. Thank you for being you, Shah Rukh.

Many look up to you for inspiration, and countless others who admire you for your craft and charm. But with me, it is different. You have touched a part of my life and soul no one else ever could. It is an unspoken and extremely intense connection that I feel with you, a vivid bond, even though it is just in my mind. If you are wondering, Shah Rukh, why I hold you in such high esteem, you may have to take a walk down the memory lane with me. I have tried to encapsulate the essence in my letters. Of course, a few humble words cannot convey the depth of my emotions for you. Consider this the beginning of a series—one that I hope you will look forward to reading as much as I enjoy writing it.

I recall something you said in one of your interviews: "*Agar aap kisi se mohabbat karte ho to kehne ki zaroorat nahi hai. Aur agar kehna pad raha hai to mohabbat nahi hai.*" [If you love someone, there is no need to say it. And if you have to say it, then it is not love].

Well, I beg to differ, Shah Rukh. Humans are not mind-readers, and we have been blessed with the ability to communicate. Why not use it? I believe if you love someone, you should tell them as many times as you can. After all, who knows, *Kal Ho Na Ho*? [What if there is no tomorrow?]

Besides, who does not love knowing that someone adores them without wanting anything in return? Be honest, Shah Rukh, don't you smile ear to ear when people scream your name with love and excitement? Of course, you do. Isn't it heart-warming to know that you matter to so many out there? I bet you are smiling right now too, as you read this letter. Hold on to that smile. Keep it intact. Millions will die for those cute little dimples. Me being one of them.

To sum it up, Shah Rukh, I am just another person whose life has been brightened by your presence. Like a warm, radiant sun, you have provided me with warmth, filling my life with joyous laughter, boundless hope, and a constant stream of inspiration. And though you may never read these words, I write them with the same love that has shaped my journey since childhood. With every letter, I invite you into my world where your movies, words, and presence have made all the difference. So, let us turn back time, rewind the memories, and relive those moments together.

Love You

Priyanka

How It All Began

Dear Shah Rukh,

1992! Yes, it was the year 1992. Do you know what happened in 1992? I turned eight. Did you think differently? Oh, you did. Do you know what else happened in 1992? I came to know about a person I was going to admire for the rest of my life. The one who was destined to take command of my heart, marking it with an unyielding seal, as if declaring, 'I rule here, and this is mine forever'. Yeah, I have known you since 1992 and have loved you ever since.

Back then, I was in second grade, full of curiosity and wonder. You were my superhero. You were the prince, and I was the princess in the fairy tales my grandma would tell me. Hugging your posters was as warm as hugging my teddy bear. I felt secure, like nothing could go wrong in my little world as long as you were there on my wall.

Does the year 1992 ring any bells for you? Yes, it does, Shah Rukh, doesn't it? But hold on, I have something to tell you first. It was neither the television nor the big screen that introduced you to me. A poster in someone's room caught my eye and when she spoke about you with so much awe and affection, I could not help but be intrigued. Shah Rukh, I thank her from the bottom of my heart for bringing you into my life.

The person who brought you into my world was my aunt. She was your huge fan and had this contagious excitement whenever your name was mentioned. I remember her gushing about a new actor who was different from the rest—someone who had this incredible charm and an infectious smile. Naturally, my eight-year-old self was intrigued. I wanted to know what all the fuss was about.

It so happened, one day, an eight-year-old me walked into my aunt's room. The room felt different. It was a complete mess. I paused for a moment and looked around to analyze what had changed. To my left, there was a wooden book rack which used to be decorated with pictures of a curly-long-haired man. Tiny bits of the scribbled-out pictures lay scattered on the floor. Paper cuttings, scissors, and glue lay on the bed. It looked like someone scraped the walls of the room. The book rack, the dressing table, and everything that once used to adorn the room looked bewildered.

Right in front of me was a poster, bigger than half my size, of an unfamiliar face staring at me from the wall. I tilted my head, looking at the poster. His cute smile and little dimples caught my attention. I gazed into his eyes for more than a minute. His hair covered most of his forehead, reaching up to his eyes. It reminded me of my favourite comic character *'Billu'*. An involuntary grin flashed across my face. I thought he was cute.

To my right was my aunt's bed. Usually, it would have the prettiest bed sheet tugged in neatly. That day, I saw newspaper clippings of the same unfamiliar face covering it. My aunt was still cutting the tiny pictures of this person from some magazines, unaware of my presence. The entire vibe of the room was different. I had never seen her room in such a mess.

"Bua," I said, "What have you done to your room? It was the most beautiful corner of our house."

The condition of the room made me uneasy. It was a tiny but the most beautifully decorated room in our house. She would reorganize her bed, dressing table and book racks every now and then to experiment with the aesthetics of the room. It smelled perfect and was a cozy and comfortable place where I would crash with her after my school. That day, it smelled of favicol and glue.

"Nothing dear, just revamping the room," she replied, placing a flock of her hair behind her ears, still busy destroying the magazines.

It was a summer afternoon. With the fan turned off and beads of sweat glistening on her forehead, she was diligently working on something important, demonstrating her commitment—or perhaps her stubbornness in the face of heat.

"But you liked the curly-long-haired man so much. Why would you take his pictures off?" I picked up a few torn pictures from the floor.

Though I was confused about what was going on, I would never miss an opportunity to tease and annoy her.

"*Mithun Chakraborty*, be respectful," she said, furrowing her brows. Her tone lacked warmth, and I understood I was not supposed to go down that road.

She immediately sensed my emotions and composed herself.

"Yes, I liked him a lot". She sighed, and then there was a sudden shift in her tone. It sounded dreamy as the next sentence slipped her lips, "But I think I am falling in love with… Shah Rukh Khan".

She flashed a picture of you and blushed, her face lighting up with the brightest smile I had ever seen. As she began telling me about you, I could not help but observe her every move. Her body language was warm and affectionate, speaking volumes about her admiration for you. She tapped her fingers excitedly, her gestures animated as she recounted your chivalry and charm. Occasionally, she would play with her hair, a subtle sign of nervous excitement, or perhaps, just her way of emphasizing a point about you.

Her speech varied in pace, quickening with enthusiasm as she described you and your impact, and then slowing down as she shared anecdotes that held special meaning for her. But what struck me the most were those moments when she would simply gaze into the distance, lost in thought, a soft smile lingering on her lips as she reflected on the joy you brought into her life.

This side of her was new to me and beyond my understanding. As a second grader, I was simply happy to see my favorite person gushing with joy. Through her words and gestures, I not only learned about you, Shah Rukh, but I also glimpsed the deep connection you forged with her heart. It was in those moments when I got to know you, Shah Rukh. An eight-year-old's curiosity sparked by her aunt's fondness, leading to a lifelong love and admiration for you.

I had never seen her like that before. It was intriguing for an eight-year-old. It was the first time I had seen her so captivated by someone. Her fascination with you fascinated me.

As of today, I do not remember the exact conversation we had, but I remember her mentioning *Circus* multiple times. Later that week, *Chitrahaar* or *Rangoli* on Door Darshan played your song, *Koi Na Koi Chahiye*. It was while watching the song that I started noticing your charm. I was mesmerized.

Shah Rukh, do you remember *Koi Na Koi Chahiye*? Oh, who am I kidding? Of course, you do. That was your entry on the big screen for the very first time. That was also your entry into my heart forever. I was fascinated. To begin with, you, the person in the song, looked adorable. You looked super cool riding that bike with the wind blowing through your hair.

Watching you smile and sing made me smile too. Your style was amazing, especially that tan-coloured jacket you wore. It was the coolest thing ever. Watching you glide through the streets; I could not help but feel a sense of wonder and admiration. Your confidence and the way you carried yourself gave off such a positive vibe. It was like you had a special kind of power that enchanted me and everyone around.

After watching that song, I started noticing bikes more often. I also became selective about the clothes I wore and paid more attention to how people looked. It was as if the song opened my eyes to a whole new world of style and appearance!

And do you know what was amazing? For the first time, I found a guy wearing a tan-coloured jacket attractive. It was like the song had a mystical effect on my perception of things. Plus, it was also the first time I realized how the wind could transform your hair into something wonderful. It was like discovering a secret about nature's beauty that I had never noticed before. It was like I was stepping into a new stage of my life, and you became the riverbank, gently guiding my free-flowing thoughts and dreams to find their way.

There was something about this song that made me feel warm and fuzzy inside, even though I could not quite figure out why. You were so charming. Everything about you in the song was so special. You were my instant favourite. I could not help but notice your smile throughout the song. Watching you was like a happy feeling that I could not explain. Whenever I looked at your posters, I beamed with joy. Even today, whenever I watch you in this song, I feel cozy and warm at heart, and it is all nostalgic.

My interests and hobbies changed with this song. All the things I used to be interested in, as a tween, did not seem as exciting anymore. Instead, I found myself drawn to something new: collecting pictures of you. It became my favourite thing to do. I made this special notebook just for your pictures, and it became my most prized possession. Hundreds of pictures of you, each one capturing a distinct memory, filled the album, and I loved them all. I maintained it for years before the smartphones came in.

Even now, that notebook remains tucked away with all my other childhood treasures at my parents' house. At night, when I climbed into bed, I would whisper to my favorite doll all about you. Talking about you with my aunt became the highlight of my day. It was like having a secret treasure to share with her.

To me, you were the most handsome and adorable person in the whole wide world, and I had the biggest crush on you. It was like having a big, innocent crush, where everything about you seemed perfect and wonderful. I was head over heels for you.

As I sit here and write these words, I cannot help but feel a huge smile spread across my face, reaching from one ear to the other. It is like I am going back in time, remembering that very first day when I discovered you. And do you know what is funny? The song *Aisi Deewangi* appears to perfectly describe my aunt's and my feelings about you. We are the two crazy ladies in our family, completely and utterly in love with everything about you.

You know Shah Rukh, that moment, that song *Koi na Koi Chaiye*, and that feeling, everything about it was special. Little did I know then that this was just the beginning of a love story that would last a lifetime. From that day forward, my world had a new meaning, a new dream, and a new name: Shah Rukh Khan. And with that, my journey of admiration had officially begun.

Love You.

Priyanka

When You Became a Part of Me

Dear Shah Rukh,

"*King of Romance!*" How did you earn that title? Hmm... Let me think. Was it a movie you were initially reluctant to do that established you as the ultimate romantic hero? Well, I am thinking of a film that is still running in theatres, and in our hearts for over three decades. I cannot quite put my finger on it. Could you help me with the name of the movie that surpasses the classic tales of Romeo and Juliet, Heer Ranjha, and Sohni Mahiwal? This love story has become the benchmark for modern couples, the gold standard that has set the bar high for guys and raised the expectations for girls. Damn it! I forgot the name. Don't just smile, help me out here, Shah Rukh!

Oh yes! *Dilwale Dulhaniya Le Jayenge*. Thank you.

You must agree Shah Rukh *DDLJ* was a turning point in your career. It is a timeless love story. The iconic characters of Raj and Simran, and not to forget Bauji, have made a place in our hearts forever. It has a cultural impact, memorable dialogues, and catchy music. It is a complete package for entertainment and an all-time favourite for everyone. *DDLJ* has been special to so many people in so many ways. I know it might sound crazy, but *DDLJ* is like a holy scripture for modern-day couples, an ultimate guide for boys and girls wanting to fall in love.

My reasons for loving this movie are slightly different, Shah Rukh. For me, it has a whole different level of value. It is extra special to me for several reasons. So, come, let us relive those moments once again. You will, for sure, see why this movie is as important to me as it is to you.

It was my twelfth birthday. My dad surprised the whole family by treating us on a trip to the movies. It was a big deal for me because I had never been to a cinema hall before. I was over the moon knowing that I was the birthday girl and that we were going to celebrate in such a special way. I considered (and still consider), myself as "*Papa ki Pari*".

I did not even bother asking which movie we were going to watch because the excitement of going to the theatre itself was enough for me. My brother and I could not contain our excitement as we got ready to leave. Dad bought us some candies and chocolates, which made the whole outing feel even more exciting and indulgent.

As we made our way to the theatre, I could not help but feel a sense of anticipation and wonder. Everything about the experience was new and thrilling. The thought of watching a movie on the big screen in a dark theatre was something of which I had always dreamed. It felt like an exciting adventure waiting to unfold, and I could not wait to see what the day had in store for us.

My first visit to the theatre was an experience I will never forget. As we approached the grand building, my eyes widened in awe at the bright marquee lights and the bustling crowd. Walking into the lobby felt like stepping into another world. The smell of freshly popped popcorn wafted through the air, mixing with the sweet scent of candies and chocolates from the concession stand.

As we settled into our seats, excitement bubbled within me, impossible to contain. The theatre was enormous, with rows of plush seats and a screen that seemed larger than life. As the lights dimmed and the screen came to life, I felt a rush of exhilaration. The booming sound, the vivid colours, and the immersive atmosphere were unlike anything I had ever experienced.

People were whistling and screaming as the movie started. My brother, sitting on my left, passed me a piece of candy. I started watching the scenes unfold on the screen. It started with an elderly gentleman. He was feeding some pigeons. It reminded me of my dad feeding our pet pigeons at home. Then there was a young girl reciting poetry to her mom. Her poetry translated into a song that echoed through the hall. People cheered and sang along. Suddenly, out of nowhere, a young boy came running with a ball, heading straight towards me.

I looked at him in utter astonishment and stood up from my chair with a jerk.

"It's him!" my voice was somewhere between a quiet whisper and a loud scream.

I was so surprised that I nearly choked on the candy. My heart skipped a beat as I whispered to myself, "Shah Rukh."

In the dim lights of the theater, as the first glimpse of you filled the screen, something inside me shifted. My breath hitched, my chest tightened, and an unfamiliar warmth spread through me, leaving me dizzy. My fingers clutched the armrest, knuckles white, as my legs trembled beneath me, unable to ground the emotions crashing over me like waves. Tears blurred my vision, but I did not wipe them away—I just stood there, utterly consumed, my heart hammering so hard it felt like the entire auditorium could hear it. I found myself shaking in disbelief. It was like a dream come true to see the person I loved the most, right there in front of me, even if it was just on the screen. It was a powerful emotion I had never felt before, a strange, beautiful pain, a mix of joy so intense that it hurt and a longing so deep that it left me breathless.

My dad, sitting to my right, sensed my emotions and gently pulled my hand. "What happened, *Beta?*" he asked.

I could not hold back my tears and said in a squeaky voice, "Why did you not tell me it was a Shah Rukh Khan movie?"

My dad teasingly responded, "If you don't like Shah Rukh, we can leave. Why waste time, right?"

I tried to argue with him, but he playfully pulled me into a hug. And that is how I ended up watching the song *Mere Khwabon Mein Jo Aye* for the first time; weeping, overwhelmed, overjoyed, and filled with so many emotions. It turned out to be a memorable experience, a mix of surprises, love, and the joy of watching something special with my family.

Throughout the film, you completely captivated me. Every scene felt real, every emotion heightened by the collective reactions of the audience. Laughter, gasps and cheers filled the theater, creating a sense of camaraderie among strangers.

I did not want the movie to end, Shah Rukh. On the big screen, you felt so close to me. You looked exceptionally outstanding. Your messy hair, naughty smile, and mischievous attitude kept me on the edge of my seat. Yet the conviction with which you loved hooked me to you forever. You had woven an irresistible pull on me, leaving me with a sense of wonder and a newfound love.

As we left the theatre, I could not stop talking about you. "Can we watch this one more time, Dad?" I would plead.

That day, you became my gateway to a world of imagination and adventure, a place where stories came to life and dreams felt within reach.

So, one reason *DDLJ* is so special to me is, this was the first movie I ever watched in a Cinema Hall. Plus, seeing you, Shah Rukh, on the big screen was a moment I will remember forever, and it made the entire experience at the movie theatre even more beautiful and unforgettable. Even as I write this today, recollecting that moment gives me goosebumps.

Twenty years later, as I sat down to watch the film again for the umpteenth time, a sudden realization struck me: "Hey, this is me, and this is my story." I noticed countless similarities between the movie and my life. The character of Simran felt like a reflection of me. It was as if I was watching my journey unfolding on the screen.

Simran resonated with me in every way imaginable. From her reluctance to entertain Raj's stupid attempts at flirting to her unshakeable trust in the one she loved; I saw echoes of my own experiences mirrored in her character. Whether it was her determination to express her desires, such as her longing for a Euro trip to her strict father, or the deeply ingrained Indian traditional values that shaped her, every aspect of her personality felt familiar to me. Everything about her felt like it could be me. It was cool to see someone so much like me in a movie.

You know Shah Rukh, whenever we talk of love stories, Raj and Simran are the perfect example. Well, believe me or not, I found my real-life Raj and married him. Mohit and my love story started off just like in the movie. I was conservative, and he was outgoing and flirtatious. I did not have many friends; he dated a dozen girls. Somehow, our paths crossed, we fell in love and eventually got married. More on that some other time.

Now here is the funny part. My father has many qualities in common with Simran's Bauji and your Pops. He had kept several pigeons as pets for years, but he was cooler than Simran's Bauji.

He was more like your Pops in the movie. Sometimes, my friends even call him *Anupam Kher!* Because of his bald head, perhaps!

Oh, and do you remember Chutki, Simran's little sister? Well, she is a lot like my younger sister, Ekta. Ekta knows all my secrets and is always there for me, just like Chutki was for Simran.

I can go on and on and on writing about you and *DDLJ*. But let me stop here for now.

DDLJ represents cherished memories and lasting inspiration to me. More than a film; it is a symbol of love, hope, and the power of dreams. It means the world to me. There has been no other movie that has come even close to *DDLJ* in terms of my liking. I had so many memories associated with this one; it was my first theatre visit, my first time seeing you on a big screen, and my twelfth birthday gift. Watching the movie over and over, I learned to dream of love and believe in them. It taught me to fall in love. Most of all, it feels like seeing myself and Mohit on screen while watching *Dilwale Dulhaniya Le Jayenge*.

In one of your interviews, I heard you were reluctant to do this movie. Really? Shah Rukh, I am forever grateful to you for making this movie and for giving us the Raj. For it is the magic of Raj that we know what love should feel like. He is the ideal of romance, showing us that love is about kindness, respect, and devotion. He made us believe in the kind of love that fights against all odds yet stays true to its values.

Shah Rukh, we owe you so much for giving us Raj and the courage to fall in love—not recklessly, but with passion, honesty, and a sense of purpose. Raj is more than just a character to us; he is a symbol of how love should be—bold, authentic, and full of meaning.

You know Shah Rukh, in the movie, the moment when you came running with a ball towards me, something stirred in me. I felt a strong emotion that I could not understand back then. At twelve, I did not have the words to name it. But today, I know. That was love.

I was falling in love with you, for the very first time. While my legs trembled, my body shivered, tears welled up in my eyes and my heart fluttered in my chest, sending a sensation down my spine. The rawness of the emotions I felt at that moment, a sense of joy, a sweet pain, the longing, and an unexplainable connection with you remains as vivid today as it was then. It felt as if time had paused just for us, and the world faded away, leaving only your smile and the sound of my racing heart. I did not fully understand it then, but in that fleeting moment, you became a part of me—a part that I knew I would carry forever.

Love You

Priyanka

Midnight Memories

Dear Shah Rukh,

Childhood days are such treasures, right? It feels so good when you stumble upon an old toy car, a half-torn comic book, or a plastic gun you used to play *Chor-Police* with. I sometimes wonder what your childhood was like. The little devil in the house or mama's boy, a tough nut to crack or a shrinking violet. What suits you more? Let us just say, you always got a simple pass, but that would be so boring. Getting your way by stomping your feet could be another sweet assumption, doesn't suit you though, for the dimples that you still have might have been more than enough to get what you wanted.

In my imagination, you were the naughtiest toddler ever running around the house on his tiny toes. You were the kid, the ladies in the neighborhood wanted to take home to play with. Well, not much has changed even today though! I think of you as the mischievous boy who could turn the house upside down and blow people's minds with his cute pranks. Okay, stop! Don't burst my bubble. This image is too cute to think otherwise.

Talking about childhood, I wanted to share a memory from my pre-teen years. As I already said, I was crazy for you and my brother, let's say, he was crazy in general. Most of the time I was the amiable chap, but my usual amiability disappeared when it came to you; my inner devil emerged. My brother, though, was constantly in the *Ugravadi* demeanour. We both had some loose screws; I can confirm this when I look back at our childhood. Just imagine the length, an otherwise quiet and innocent seventh grader, who was infatuated with you, would go, just to watch your movies.

Even though I was mostly a quiet and obedient child, every time I heard about your new release, my inner imp came alive. I would leave no stone unturned to catch you at the cinema. I would ask my parents to take me to the movie and stop having my meals if they disagreed. To get to the cinema, I would abandon my homework and throw tantrums. That's how kids are: problematic!

I would beg, plead, throw tantrums, and do everything in my power to convince my parents to take me to the theatre or rent a cassette to watch your movie. Whether I heard about it from friends, saw it in the newspaper, or caught your new song on TV or radio, I was eager to watch the movie from start to finish. I used to create a checklist of your movies and eagerly waited to tick each one off.

However, we were a middle-class family, and for us, visits to cinemas were reserved for special occasions, birthdays and other family outings. I can actually count on my fingers the number of movies I have watched in a theatre since my first movie encounter until I got married.

We did not go to the cinema often. Instead, we relied on Door Darshan. We eagerly awaited weekends when Door Darshan aired a few movies. We also looked forward to the movies shown by our local cable providers. The cable provider was our best bet to catch the latest movies.

With school, homework, and exams, there was hardly any free time left. I cannot even count how many exams schools used to throw at us. Seriously, who thought that was a good idea? The main area of focus in every middle-class family is education. Now I understand it was important, but back then, I could only curse God for creating schools and teachers for giving us exams. Now, I know, life gives us more tests than those we took in schools!

Amidst these class tests, unit tests, and half-yearly and annual exams, Mom would often limit our TV sessions, sometimes for the sake of our education and sometimes because of the low and fluctuating voltage supply.

Despite these challenges, I would never pass up the chance to watch your movies. It was not easy, but whenever a Shah Rukh Khan movie aired, I would make sure to catch it. Even though we could not go to the cinema as much as we'd liked and had to balance schoolwork with leisure time, your movies were something I always looked forward to.

And you know Shah Rukh, your movies and songs were the one thing my parents used as bait to keep me moving towards my goals or their goals, probably.

"You want to see a Shah Rukh Khan movie? We want a hundred per cent mark in your math exam. Is that a deal?"

"Make your room and you can go watch your weekend Shah Rukh Khan movie."

"We are going out. Take care of your little brother. We will watch a Shah Rukh Khan's movie as soon as we return."

I mean, if there was an award for manipulating your kids to do what you want, I am sure my parents would be the best contestant. But they always fulfilled their promises and my desires. After every deal they made with me, irrespective of the results, they would always allow me to watch your movies. It was my accolade for trying. We watched movies like *Raju Ban Gaya Gentleman, Chamatkar, Kabhi Haan Kabhi Na* et cetera. on TV.

Then came your *Dil to Pagal Hai*. My friends and cousins would talk about it nonstop. They would discuss the songs, some scenes, and your quirky dialogues. Despite my eagerness to join in on their discussions, I felt left out. However, I had heard so much about it from others that I could practically visualize the movie without ever having watched it. The city was dancing to the tunes of the soundtracks from the movie. One or the other song from the movie was always on my lips. You were always in my thoughts. Every time the name *Dil to Pagal Hai* popped up, I felt a pang of longing. It was like I was missing out on something important.

This time, I feared asking my dad to take us to the movies. He was very particular about our studies, and it was our final exam. No one would take you to the movie during your exams, right?

It was the month of March. The weather was cold. We used to study in our drawing room and my mom kept a close eye on us. We followed an exam ritual during that period. During our exams, we slept around 8 pm. Dad would wake us at 4 am. He would give us a test paper to solve. He would prepare the test paper himself. This was his way of making us do a final revision before we left for school by 6:30 am. This had been a routine in our family for years. I now wonder how many exam papers my dad would have created, every year, every subject, and for two kids.

I remember it was my chemistry paper the next day. A subject I still dread of. That day, my little brother fell asleep in the drawing room. Mom asked me too, to sleep there, to avoid any scares if he woke up at night. When she said that, a spark of excitement lit up inside me. Sleeping in the drawing room meant one thing: movie night! I could barely hold my excitement as I waited for them to leave the room.

Once Mom and Dad left the room, I shut the door, turned off the lights, and switched on the TV, keeping the sound on mute. As I flipped through the channels, a wave of guilt washed over me.

"I should be sleeping, if not studying," I thought.

"Let me watch TV for thirty minutes and then I will be back studying," I promised myself.

I started memorizing the periodic table and some chemical formulas while scrolling the channels and there you were, on one of them. My search stopped. I found what I was looking for. It was like finding a hidden treasure.

It was one fateful night. Luck smiled upon me as the cable provider aired *Dil To Pagal Hai*. The excitement bubbling inside me was impossible to contain. I had been longing to watch this movie ever since I saw you on the posters throughout the city.

However, I was in a dilemma. My parents had trusted me to sleep while I was ready to watch a movie. Then again, Chemistry Vs Shah Rukh Khan or Chemistry with Shah Rukh Khan. The choice was not an easy one.

I calculated, 'If I don't score well in this exam, I cannot watch this movie', that was the deal with Dad. But the chances of me scoring well in chemistry were bleak.

'If I don't watch it now, and study the entire night, the current level of preparation will not suffice. Ultimately, this is my only chance to watch this movie,' I convinced myself.

It is so easy to give in to temptations, Shah Rukh. You will always find a reason to justify your actions. Consoling my heart, I went for the movie. But there was a problem. The TV was on mute. How could I possibly enjoy this on mute? And a higher volume would certainly wake my parents up.

So, I inched towards the TV, so close that I could see every pixel on the screen. The screen light flashed my face in a soft glow, and I could feel a bit of warmth from the electronics. It was like I had stepped into the TV world itself, surrounded by the action and drama unfolding just inches from my nose. I cranked up the volume to a daring level of 1, just enough that it felt like you were whispering in my ears and started my movie adventure from a mere foot away from the TV.

As I watched, I could not take my eyes off you. You were my heartthrob. You were adorable. Your dimples deepened as you flashed a mischievous grin, eyes twinkling with a charm that could soften even the sternest faces. The way you tilted your head slightly while smiling made me feel a warm, fuzzy affection. Your laugh was infectious and had a way of lighting up the room, drawing me in effortlessly.

Honestly, Shah Rukh, I was not watching the movie that day. How do you expect me to watch a movie at such low volumes? I was watching you. The way you walked, your body language, your expressions, your charisma, I started noticing everything about you. The expression when you hide your genuine emotions, those eyes that speak volumes and that smile that can pierce any heart, I saw you very closely that day. Yeah, just one foot away from the TV, remember!

Hey, don't laugh, Shah Rukh, I have more to tell.

Lost in your thoughts, I did not notice the passing hour. I did not realize that my legs had frozen in the chilling winter until a sudden footstep broke the spell. Panic surged through me. I feared I had been caught.

The only thought on my mind was, "That's it. I am going to get thrashed today."

I turned off the TV, drew the TV cover as fast as I could, jumped onto the sofa and pretended to be fast asleep.

Dad stepped into the room, and, despite my best efforts to fake sleep, he seemed to know I had been up to something. I don't know how he knew. It could have been my devil brother, but he came straight to me. Probably, parents have a sixth sense for their children.

With a gentle pat on my head, he asked, "Were you watching TV?" I opened my eyes slowly. His gaze locked onto me. He had that look, the one that said he knew what I had been up to. Fear gripped me. I was on the verge of crying. Perhaps my dad sensed it because he did not scold me. Instead, he inquired about what I was watching; and asked me to sleep for the upcoming exam the next day. I wondered how patient he was.

You know Shah Rukh; kids are manipulative too. You give them an inch, and they will take a mile. That day, my father stayed calm, and I took advantage of the situation. I pulled him into sweet talking, or so I thought.

I squared my shoulders and took a deep breath, the words stumbling out nervously, "Would you... um, maybe want to watch this movie?"

He looked at me in disbelief. "You know, today is crucial for your exams. Movies can wait; your exam will not."

I was so hooked on you, Shah Rukh, that I argued with my dad. I assured him I was well prepared, praying to God that he should not quiz me right now on some chemical formula. After an extensive debate, he trying to convince me to sleep and me trying to convince him to complete Shah Rukh Khan's movie; I won. He sat beside me, and we watched the rest of the movie together.

Once the movie finished, he tugged me into the bed and moved out of the room. It was already 12:30 am. I could not sleep though. The guilt and the lack of preparation for the exam made me uneasy. I woke up again, pulled out my notes and a torch and sat in my quilt revising.

I don't remember when I dozed off, but when I woke up, my notebook was on the table alongside the torch, and I was warm in my blanket. It was a pleasant surprise that there were no early wake-up calls for me. Dad simply said, "Don't stress, you will do well. All the best," as I left for school. Surprisingly, I did well and passed with flying colours.

The exams went well, but I kept pondering how my dad knew I was watching TV. How he knew it was me and not my naughty little brother. A few days later, when I could not contain my curiosity anymore, I asked my father, "How did you know I was watching TV that night?"

He looked at me, smiled, and buried his face behind the newspaper as he continued reading it.

"Dad??" I asked again.

He tilted his head to his left, moving the newspaper to the other side, still smiling.

"*Stabilizer on tha*," he winked.

"Why do we use stabilizers?" I murmured to myself.

"And how were you so sure it was me? It could have been Varun." My curiosity was clear in my words.

He chuckled and walked away. Puzzled, I asked, "Dad?"

As if reading all the questions on my face, he sighed and replied, "The cable provider came for his monthly payment that day. He boasted about your Shah Rukh a lot. He also confirmed that he would show his latest release that night. What are the odds?"

I did not know what to curse more, the fluctuating voltage supply compelling us to use the stabilizer or the cable provider to brag about you. I was still processing the thoughts when my dad smiled and patted my head.

"Looks like your Shah Rukh is gaining popularity. People are really fond of him." His words made me smile.

This was a small incident, Shah Rukh, but a memorable one. Unknowingly, I learned some valuable lessons. It taught me the importance of balancing work and leisure.

They say that *All work and no play makes Jack a dull boy*. Well, I lived by the saying that night. I learned to sneak in fun in stressful times. Little breaks during our most demanding and nerve-wracking situations go a long way. Even today, when I am overly frustrated, I take a small break, go for a walk, call a friend or make a shopping list and all frustration starts to melt away.

The incident reinforced the idea that honest and open communication between a child and parents can lead to better outcomes. Imagine if my dad had screamed at me instead of being calm and patient that night, our dynamics would have been different. I would have gone to bed scared of Dad and sad to have missed your movie. I would have been angry in the morning and cursing my father and probably that mood would have had its effect on my exam as well. But nothing of that sort happened because my dad not only listened but also joined in with me, understanding my emotions. It deepened my admiration for my dad.

Looking back, that night was more than just a stolen movie moment. It was a lesson in finding joy even in the smallest rebellions. It taught me that passion and responsibility can coexist, that a little rule-breaking for what we love makes life more beautiful, and most importantly, that my father was way cooler than I had ever imagined.

And you, Shah Rukh? You weren't just a film on my screen that night. And since I observed you so closely, from barely a foot away, you got engraved in my heart forever. That moment was not just a childhood memory, it was the beginning of a lifelong love story, written in the glow of a screen, whispered in the quiet thrill of the night.

Love You,

Priyanka

The Shah Rukh Khan Effect

Dear Shah Rukh,

Did you ever have sibling squabbles as a kid? Well, with the picture I have painted in my imagination of your childhood, you must have been a handful for everyone around you. I am sure you would have irritated and annoyed your sister over trivial matters. That's what brothers are for! They fight over stupid things just to irritate their sisters!

But tell me one thing, who usually won those fights? How many times have your parents stepped in to settle the dispute and whose side do they tend to take? For me, even now, one of the greatest agonies of life is when my parents and relatives play the '*You are older. Let it go*' game or '*He is your younger brother. Let it be*' line. It was exasperating back then, and it is just as frustrating now. I mean, *hadd hai yar*!

Let me share a bit about my family. My dad worked for a nationalized bank. My mother, once a lecturer, switched her job to a full-time child trainer when I was born and refuses to retire even now. I am the eldest of my siblings. My brother, Varun, is two and a half years younger than me, and my sister, Ekta, who is more like a daughter to me, is twelve years younger. Now, don't get me wrong, we have a strong bond that nothing can break. But, oh boy, when we were kids, we used to fight like cats and dogs sometimes!

We were like *Tom and Jerry*, who could not live with each other and could not live without each other. There were days when one would pass their piece of cake to the other selflessly, and then there were days when even the grapes were counted and shared. Some days we would be at each other's throats and some days nobody could come between us.

Most of the time, our fights were about silly stuff. Like, who gets to sleep closest to the cooler on hot summer nights, or who gets the last *Aam ki Guthli*, or even stuff like, "Why are you reading so loudly? I cannot concentrate on my homework!" And oh, the classic one, "Your Shah Rukh looks like a chipmunk!" Can you believe it, Shah Rukh?

I am sure, being a dad of three, you have had your fair share of similar situations in your family too, right? No, don't lie. Aaryan and Suhana are well-groomed and well-mannered, but I could bet that as kids if you left them in a room alone, they would surely find a reason to make you go nuts. It is all part of growing up and learning to live with each other's quirks and differences.

Hey, I just realized the age difference between your kids is similar to what my siblings and I have. Hence, I can speculate that Aryan and Suhana are your Tom and Jerry just like me and Varun and Abram is the most pampered kid in your family, and so is Ekta.

Anyway, among all these truffles between me and Varun, the most frequent one was fighting over the TV. And here is a story about one such fight we had.

One bright Sunday morning, I settled into my favourite spot on the couch, my eyes glued to the TV screen as one of my absolute favourites *Tum Pas Aye* played. I swayed slightly, lost in the rhythm, feeling a rare moment of happiness.

There is something about you, Shah Rukh. Whenever I watch you, I feel joyful. A smile spreads across my face and warmth in my heart at the mere mention of your name. You are my happy hormones.

So, while I was lost in the song, replacing Rani Mukherjee with myself in my mind, Varun jumped in from God knows where and flipped the channel to some sports channel. My heart sank and my joy vanished in an instant.

"What on earth! I was watching the song!", I protested, reaching out for the remote.

"It is match day today, India Vs South Africa," he replied, raising the remote over my head. With a smug grin on his face he continued, "No more stupid SRK songs for today".

My face flushed with anger. "Don't you dare say anything about Shah Rukh!"

Varun just laughed and ignored me while his eyes were still glued to the TV screen. I tried to snatch the remote from him but could not get it. Meanwhile, he kept making silly faces and swaying the remote in the air over my head. He kept screaming. "Shah Rukh is a Chipmunk!"

I was turning red, my hands balling into a fist and before long, we were yelling and pulling each other's hair.

Dad walked into the room, his face a mix of confusion and annoyance. "What is wrong with the two of you? Who fights like this?"

We both tried to explain what had just happened, our voices overlapping. It was like a debate on Shah Rukh Khan Vs Jonty Rhodes.

Dad listened, then sighed. "*Tum badi ho na, chote bhai se aise nai ladte, jane do*", came the classic reply. " It's just a song. Shah Rukh's song isn't going anywhere," he said casually.

Varun always teased me about you just to get on my nerves, but when my father uttered those words, " Shah Rukh's song isn't going anywhere", I was taken aback. I could not bear it. My father's casual dismissal stung more than any harsh word could.

No offence to anyone, and even though it was like comparing apples to oranges, I could not accept that my father thought Mr. Jonty Rhodes was more worthy than my Shah Rukh Khan. No one understood my love for you.

I felt the familiar weight of dejection settle over me. I stood there, feeling a lump in my throat, my eyes stinging with tears. Varun always got away with things because he was younger, and I was expected to be the bigger person. It wasn't just about the song; it was about feeling invisible and unimportant.

I was frustrated because no one ever considered my perspective or feelings equally. I felt my opinion never mattered. It was unfair. And to top that, I never dared to express these emotions honestly. Every time I tried to speak, my words seemed to disappear into thin air. I feared my feelings would be dismissed and invalidated. I felt I had no self-esteem or importance in the family. It was as if in my own home, my desires and feelings came second because I was "elder" and a "girl". Perhaps, Shah Rukh, at a subconscious level, this could have been my fear of not being heard and understood because that day my dad's words cut deep.

That day, it was the last straw. It was too much to handle and before I knew, a tear rolled down my cheek as I shouted, "It's not just a song!" I screamed, my voice trembling with raw emotions.

"And why does being older matter?" My fists clenched as I fought to keep my composure.

Varun's eyes widened in surprise. My father looked at me, stunned by my outburst. I had never raised my voice like this before.

"Shah Rukh means everything to me!" I continued, my voice shaking but determined. "He makes me feel happy and seen. When I watch him, it's like he is telling me it is okay to dream and be myself. But you don't get it. You don't value him like I do, and it hurts."

My father frowned, still not understanding the depth of my feelings.

I turned to my brother, "Even if it is a repeat telecast of Sri Lanka and Australia's match at 2 a.m., he wants to watch it and no one has a problem with that. All I wanted was to see a two-minute Shah Rukh Khan song. Was it such a big deal, dad?" I looked my father in his eyes.

"What happened? Are you alright?" my father's face softened, realizing that my outburst was more than just about a song. He saw the hurt in my eyes, the vulnerability I tried so hard to hide.

"It's not just a song!" I continued, my voice shaking, but determined. "You don't get it, do you? It is never just about the song!" I cried. "Every time I want something, it's always *'tum badi ho, Bhai hai tumhara, jane do'*. But it is never about what I want!"

"You always tell me to be the bigger person," I said, tears brimming in my eyes. "But I feel like I am always the one giving up what I love. And no one even cares!"

I paused, my breath coming in shaky gasps. The unspoken pain, the years of feeling overlooked and unheard, finally boiled over.

"Why does everything I love have to come second to everyone else? Why can't you see how much this means to me?" I continued, " It is not fair!"

"Do I even matter in this house? Am I invisible? Do I have any value for anyone, Dad?".

With tears streaming down my face, I turned my gaze to Varun in anguish, "*Khush ho na, ghar k shehzade*" (Yeah, my brother's pet name is Prince). I tossed the remote on the sofa and stomped out of the room.

Feeling overwhelmed with emotions, I retreated to my room. I flopped down onto my bed and buried my face in a pillow, whimpering. A few minutes later the faint tones of, *Na jane Kaisa ehsaas hai*, echoed in the air. For a moment, I thought it was playing in my mind. But when the volume grew louder, I dashed out of the room, drawn by the familiar tune. To my surprise, I found my father tuning in to Vividh Bharati on the radio, and by sheer luck, the song I needed to hear was playing. With a knowing smile, my dad turned up the volume to its fullest.

The song filled the room with its touching melody. At that moment, as I felt choked up, the music brought me comfort and made me feel understood.

Later in the evening, my dad came over and sat down to talk to me about what I had mentioned earlier. He listened to me, paying close attention to everything I had to say. It was like he wanted to understand all the feelings I had been carrying around, even though I was still young. For the first time, I felt like someone truly heard me and understood what I was going through. It was a special moment that made me see just how much my dad cared about me.

A few days later, it was Raksha Bandhan, and my brother surprised me with a mixed tape filled with your songs. As I unwrapped the package, I noticed the words written on it: *Dekho ye pagli, bilkul na badli*. It was his playful way of saying, "I love you." The gift meant so much to me because it showed that he remembered my love for you and took the time to create something special just for me. He grasped a part of me that others overlooked, making the gift carry an even deeper significance. Every time I listen to those songs, I feel a connection not just with you, Shah Rukh, but also with my brother and the strong bond we share.

After that incident, something significant changed within our family dynamics. My parents never used the "*Tum badi ho*" phrase again. Not only did they refrain from using such phrases, but they also began to stand up for me whenever someone else dared to utter them. They did not just talk about "Equality between sons and daughters", it reflected in their actions too. My brother's behaviour towards me changed, too. He started treating me with more gentleness, greater kindness, and consideration, prioritizing my feelings above his own.

It dawned on me that my family had recognized the emotional toll those words had taken on me. It was through your influence, Shah Rukh, I found the courage to assert myself and express my emotions, which led to a deeper level of acceptance, love, and gentleness within our family. Your presence changed our family for the better and that is what my brother termed as "The Shah Rukh Khan Effect."

In conclusion, Shah Rukh, your impact not only added joy to my life through your movies but also transformed our family bonds. You were never just an actor in my life. You were the bridge that helped me find my voice, the unspoken connection that taught my family to listen.

Your influence made us understand each other better, fostering a deeper sense of harmony and love within our family. You have been a significant part of my journey, shaping moments both big and small, and bringing countless positive changes into my life. Your presence has truly made a difference, Shah Rukh.

My brother was right, this was 'The Shah Rukh Khan Effect.' And it is a force, a *mantra* that has stayed with us ever since.

Love You

Priyanka

Butterflies in Stomach

Dear Shah Rukh,

I wanted to share with you today something that is both a cherished memory and a little piece of my heart. It is about the first time I was attracted to someone other than you. I bet you would still have the feeling of your very first crush fresh in your heart, a mix of excitement, nervousness and endless day dreaming. For me, it was all that and more, and I think you'd enjoy hearing the story of how it all began.

Whenever we speak of love and romance, my thoughts always revolve around you. But then there is this little piece of my mind that drifts back to that first innocent spark, the one that made my heart race and brought a shy smile to my face. It was my very first crush, a feeling so pure and new that it still holds a special place in my memories.

I had a crush, other than you, while in school. Even though he did not have your dimples, he had quite the charm. Let me tell you about the guy who tried to steal your girl. The one who made an impudent effort to compete with you. Oh, who am I kidding? No one can take your place in my heart.

Being in love is an amazing feeling. It feels like a rush of a cool breeze on a warm sunny day. You would not miss any opportunity to steal a glance at them, and every glimpse of them makes your heart flutter. Your lips stretch to form a pleasant curve on your face every time you think of them, a smile that will not fade away. When they are around, you feel warm inside; you are filled with a sense of calm yet thrilling excitement. It feels like you have discovered a missing piece of your soul in them, and everything falls into place perfectly.

Their laughter lingers in the air, echoing in your mind long after they have gone. It is like the sweetest melody you have ever heard, and you cannot help but beam out of joy. A simple touch from them is like a current of electricity, sparking life into every corner of your being. In those moments, you realize that love is not just a feeling, it is a blend of sensations that add beauty and meaning to your life.

Am I sounding like a love-stricken poet? Well, I am not a poet, but I would agree I was smitten with love. You know what it feels like to be truly in love. Of Course, you do! Shah Rukh, you are the king of romance. Who would know more than you? You have given us a lot many love stories on screen. But my favorite one is your real-life love story. I have heard about it in your interviews, and it is the sweetest thing ever. I am sure you would have felt the butterflies in your stomach too when you first met the love of your life. Love is a beautiful feeling, and it is difficult to forget your first love experience.

Okay Shah Rukh, tell me this: did your heart skip a beat when you first saw Gauri Ma'am? Something inside you must have stirred at that moment. Was it her laughter that caught your attention, or her smile that lingered in your memory long after? I can imagine there was nervous excitement within you, a haste to ask her out yet something holding you back. I bet you would have gone through the "to be or not to be" state where your heart wanted to woo her, but your mind told you to stay within your limits. You must have rehearsed what to say several times before approaching her. Your palms must have been sweaty, and your heart beating louder than ever. You must have tried to hold your composure while your legs shook in your boots. The uncertainty of her response would have made you lose your night's sleep.

I am sure you remember how it felt when you fell in love with Gauri Ma'am, and you recall what it was like to be head over heels for someone. She must have been your inspiration to, let's say, show up early where you had always been late, or attend an event that you had denied going out with friends saying it was not your type. She might have been a reason for you to do something you hated. I know it is been quite some time for you and Gauri Ma'am, but the feeling of first love is unforgettable.

Bet me if you want, but I believe you still remember what she was wearing and how she looked and smiled when you first saw her. You probably recall many details from your first date. During those times, did the butterflies not flutter and swirl in your stomach? They did, didn't they?

Today, I want to share with you a time when I felt those same butterflies in my stomach. Let us go back to the years 2000 to 2001, which are special to me in several ways. I turned sixteen; I was getting ready for my board exams and had started to develop feelings for a guy at school. And as if you knew exactly what I needed, you released Mohabbatein. A story which filled the air with love.

Teenage years are special, but sweet sixteen holds a unique significance for a girl. It marks her transition from childhood to adolescence. For me, it was a pivotal moment in my life. With hormones in full swing, I often found myself gazing into the mirror, admiring my beauty, talking to my reflection in the mirror. Singing and dancing to the tunes of your songs for hours was yet another favourite activity I was found indulged in. I started developing an interest in poetry, and the words I read on paper came alive in my imagination. At sixteen, I wrote my first poem for you. I had woven my own dreamland, and you were a significant part of it.

With everything else came newfound freedoms and responsibilities. The first challenge I faced at sixteen was my board exams, staring at me, right in my face. It was such a phobia. Schools, coaching classes, self-assessments, pre-boards, lab practicals and much more. It was an overwhelming challenge for someone who had been carefree just a year earlier.

Everyone around me spoke only about how crucial the board's exams were. My parents made sure we had a hundred per cent attendance in class. The teachers were rushing us to complete the course so that we could have some time for revision. Friends and classmates were busy solving the previous year's exam papers. And as if this was not enough, every time a relative showed up at home, they would have a grin on their face which was far from being a happy smile, it was more of a sarcastic smirk, while they asked, "How is your preparation going?" or gave comments like, "Don't worry, you will rock your boards". I never understood what interest the world had in my performance in the board exams. They just made it a horrifying experience for me.

Anyway, the year flew by in a blur, swept up in the rush of academic pressures. But the one thing I liked about being sixteen was a guy from school. Oh, whenever I think of him, I want to be sixteen again. He was of average height, with his complexion and build resembling that of Mr. R Madhvan from *RHTDM—Rehna Hai Tere Dil Me*.

Having a blend of academic excellence and athletic skills, he was an all-rounder. and a teacher's pet. He was either found on the first bench of the class or playing football on the playground. From scoring the top position in Math's Olympiad to winning the interschool football match and from representing our school in the national science fair to volunteering for community services, his name was in every nook and corner of the school.

Boys like him usually have a huge fan following and so had he. He was two years senior to me and girls from my class admired him a lot. It was so bad they had to call him *'Bhaiya'*.

I first took notice of him while standing in the assembly line for our morning prayer, where he was announced as our school captain. Amidst the cheering and hooting, I saw a guy a little taller than me emerging from the crowd. His hair was neatly combed in a side parting. In a perfectly ironed school uniform, with a tie and a blazer, he looked cute, with a determined glint in his eyes. He moved swiftly, in each step, he exuded the confidence of a schoolboy who knew he belonged at the top. As he walked up the stage, his lips curved into a broad smile, his eyes sparkling with pride and joy. The corners of his mouth stretched upward, revealing a row of gleaming teeth. His entire face lit up, radiating happiness and accomplishment, as he accepted the position with a gracious nod.

There was something about his eyes and the way he spoke, or perhaps his voice and demeanour, that enchanted me. Although I could only admire him from a distance, I felt an immediate connection. As he received his captain's badge and delivered his speech, I could only gaze at him. It evoked emotions that I never knew existed in me.

Shah Rukh, you know, at a subconscious level, the human brain is aware of and can sense if someone is staring at them or they are being watched. Perhaps because of this awareness, our new school captain glanced in my direction, and at that moment, our eyes met for the first time. It felt as though I was entering a new world, much like when Sleeping Beauty was awakened by the prince's touch. In my fantasy world, he became a welcomed addition.

You know, Shah Rukh, I feel an incredibly deep connection with you, as if you have been there with me at every significant stage of my life—holding my hand and guiding me through. It is almost as though we are connected by some universal force because whenever I find myself in doubt or facing a dilemma, you somehow show me a sign. At sixteen, when I was brimming with the excitement and innocence of first love, it felt like you understood exactly how I felt. And then, as if perfectly timed, you released Mohabbatein, complementing my emotions and giving me a language to express what I could not put into words.

Mohabbatein was brimming with love stories and heartfelt moments that made everyone swoon. As a teenager with a crush, watching the characters on screen fall in love was both exhilarating and calming. While three couples were entwined in their romances, I found myself most drawn to Mr. Raj Aryan, and you will soon understand why.

Cupid's arrow had found its mark—I was hopelessly attracted to our head boy at school. He became my reason for eagerly showing up to school every day, transforming a once mundane routine into an exciting anticipation. Going to school had never been so exciting before. Perhaps he was the reason for my hundred per cent attendance in that academic session.

The moment I stepped into the school premises, my eyes would search for him. During the assembly, while everyone else prayed, I kept looking at him from the corners of my eyes, while avoiding the teachers' gaze. At recess, I would find a place outside my classroom from where I could look at him, while my friends talked about - I don't remember what, as everything else would fade away. My participation in the Olympiads, exhibitions and extracurricular activities increased as it gave me a chance to stay around him.

From the grey-coloured Milton water bottle, he carried to the way he slung his bag on his left shoulder; I noticed every detail with keen interest yet never found the courage to approach him. My state of mind was such that when you sang *Aankhe Khuli ho Ya ho Band*, it felt like you had peered into my soul and were reciting my exact feelings.

Then came the Youth Festival, a time for celebration and showcasing talents. The organizers divided the students into three houses: red, blue, and green, creating an inter-house competition. My class teacher and the dance teacher motivated me to take part in the dance competition. I was hesitant at first, but when I realized he was in the same house and was taking part in some events, I seized the opportunity. This meant during the practice hours, I could be in his proximity. Being around him was my ultimate motivation.

During practice sessions, I was more focused on what he was up to. Who was he talking to and what was the conversation about? I tried to deduce his likes and dislikes by just being around him. I learned he had a keen interest in Cricket, and *Ajay Jadeja* was his favourite cricketer. He liked Mathematics and Chemistry more than any other subject and his favourite dessert was *Kheer*. Occasionally, our eyes would meet, and I would look away coyly. At times, we smiled at each other, but words remained unspoken.

On the big day, participants gathered backstage, waiting for their turn to perform. It was a confined area, and we all stood close to each other. While my eyes were searching for him, he came and stood next to me, just inches away. It was close enough that he could probably sense my heartbeat or could feel my breath. While engrossed in a conversation with another team member, his hands brushed against mine. I am not sure if it was intentional or accidental, but it sent a shiver down my spine. My body reacted with a rush of adrenalin. I trembled for a second and I could feel my blood rushing to my head, leaving my feet and palms cold while my face radiated the warmth.

I felt intoxicated by his mere presence, my stomach fluttering with nervous excitement. The butterflies in my stomach were very prominent at that moment.

The day flew by, and I could only steal glances at him while he performed on the stage. When the results were announced, I won a second prize for solo dance performance while he excelled in various events, securing a first place in the speech and debate, and second in the fashion show.

After the event, summoning all my courage, I approached him.

"Hey!" I said, trying hard to control my voice from stammering. I could not call him by his name as he was a senior and addressing him *'Bhaiya'* was out of the question.

"Hi Priyanka!" he replied, his eyes shrunk as a curve formed on his face. His voice vibrated as he called out my name. Hearing him say my name made my breath catch, or should I say the way he pronounced my name, made my stomach do flips, and I felt a surge of warmth spread from my chest. Coming out of his mouth, my name felt divine and special.

"Congratulations." I extended my hand, still trying not to shiver.

He shook my hand, "Thank You".

He did not let go of my hand. When his sturdy yet gentle hands enveloped mine, my breath caught in my throat. For a moment, I wondered how perfectly our hands fit with each other.

He paused for a moment and, as if recollecting something, he squeezed my hand gently, "Hey, congratulations to you too. You were amazing". His hands were warm while mine were cold. As he held my hand, a gentle warmth spread from his fingers, moving up my arm and filling my whole body. I could feel my pulse quicken, and a soft flush crept up my cheeks.

That first touch was amazing. The warmth of his hand, the shared moment, felt like a scene from a movie. The melody of *Humko hum hi se chura lo* played in my mind long after. For hours later, I kept looking at my hand, touching my cheeks and humming this song, trying to re-live the two-minute connection we shared.

His gentle reciprocation gave me a positive vibe. Now we would often smile at each other from a distance. I noticed that he would also look around for me if I was not present, but we never spoke much. I would occasionally create fake problems, academically though, that I could use as an excuse to speak to him. After all, he was the district topper. He would also put in his time and best efforts to explain and help me solve those. It was silly that we both (I assume) were brimming with similar emotions but kept it within limits. In today's time, we may call that professional!

Those were the only conversations we ever had before he graduated and left school, leaving behind memories of our brief connection. His memories, the feelings he evoked in me stayed with me for over a decade. The way Raj Aryan loved her girlfriend who was not in the world, I liked this guy who was miles apart and God knows where on this earth. The greatest mystery of my life is that I never had a clue whether he had the slightest idea of my feelings for him, though I want to assume he did.

"*Toh kya hua, agar woh tumse pyaar nahi karti? Tumne usse pyaar karne se pehle yeh shart to nahi rakhi thi, ki woh bhi tumse pyaar kare. Pyaar me shartein nai hoti.*"

These lines echoed within me for years and those feelings for him lingered throughout my teenage years and beyond.

Although Shah Rukh, I had feelings for this school time crush over several years, I often found myself caught in a chaos of conflicting emotions. There was so much confusion in my mind about my own feelings. I felt enveloped with guilt. A guilt of being a betrayer. Despite my constant and everlasting devotion to you, I felt a nagging sense of regret creep in whenever thoughts of him surfaced. It felt like I was betraying my connection with you, as if every smile exchanged with him echoed a silent apology to you.

Standing in front of the mirror, I would stare at my reflection, struggling with self-condemnation. "You are being bad, terrible, girl," I would whisper, trying to reconcile the inexplicable attraction pulling me away from you. I felt I was cheating on you. Your pictures in my notebook became both a shrine to our love and a canvas for my guilt-ridden confessions. I would speak to those images, pleading for forgiveness, reaffirming my undying love for you, all while wrestling with the turmoil inside.

There have been nights that I cried when I could not understand why my heart was attracted to someone else but you. The confusion, the longing, the devotion I had for you, it all seemed so overwhelming—as if I was caught between two worlds. My inner conflict, my battle between loyalty and the unfamiliar pull of attraction elsewhere, left me torn.

Shah Rukh, adolescent love, is supposed to be pure and uncomplicated. But for me, it felt like a maze of emotions I was struggling to navigate. I was so confident about my passion for you that when these new feelings erupted, I felt strange and scared. The intensity of those emotions was so overwhelming at times that I thought there was something seriously wrong with me. I felt frustrated with the complexities of growing up and the turbulent path of love.

Now when I think about those days, Shah Rukh, I cannot help but laugh at my teenage antics. I realize how charmingly naïve I was. But hey! Teenage is a difficult phase of our life and our first loves and crushes are like the sweetest comedies we star in during our youth. They are like badges of honour we wear throughout life. We act foolishly, we overthink every glance, every word and every touch. But in the end, these moments are precious, leaving us with memories that make us smile. Silly, adolescent love!

So that was about my first attraction towards someone other than you. But I was not the only one feeling love in the air. There were others too. Every time I went up to the terrace, my neighbour's son would blast the Mohabbatein tape at full volume and gaze at me from across his terrace.

Another guy, staying as a paying guest in the lodge across from our house, would follow me to the bus stop and throw love letters wrapped around little pebbles.

Yet another guy followed me to my coaching classes and asked me out for coffee with a note written on a Peepal leaf. I am sure my brother would have thrashed him black and blue, as I never saw him again after that incident.

Being sixteen was tough. I had a strange feeling that somehow, I had become a queen of hearts for so many in the neighborhood. It was as if love was swirling around everywhere, and I found myself caught in the middle of it all. Each encounter was both flattering and overwhelming.

Looking back, I realize what a deadly combination it was: being sixteen, first crush, Mohabbatein, and board exams all at once. It was a whirlwind of emotions and excitement, with love and exams colliding in unexpected ways.

In all this chaos, *Mohabbatein* proved to be a saviour for me. The movie was all about love. Your encouragement in every scene made me want to fall in love. I wished to feel loved. Every time a song from the movie played, I could only think of the guy from school, and then the image would slowly translate to you. I was so engrossed in those thoughts that one day while riding my bicycle to my coaching class, I almost caused an accident.

While on the way, thinking about you, the familiar strains of *Humko Humhi Se Chura Lo* echoed in the air. I had a flash that you were right in front of me. I hit the brakes very hard, causing the cycle to halt immediately, and a scooter slammed into it, leading to a traffic jam. People started yelling at me. I crawled my cycle aside, smiled and thought, "*Chalte Chalte Kahi Ruk Jati hu Main*"

That was the effect you had on me, Shah Rukh, and I am sure several others would concur with me that sweet sixteen was never just an age; it was a feeling, a moment suspended in time. Love was all around, yet the true understanding of it was something we rarely learned in school.

And so, we turned to you. Both you and Mohabbatein not only marked a significant chapter of my teenage years but also became a timeless reminder of the power of deep emotions. You have a huge role in shaping my understanding and experience of heartfelt connections. Your portrayal of love, with all its joys, challenges, and emotions, has been elemental in helping me process this complex feeling.

We don't have books and courses to understand the complexities of love. We have you. You helped us explore and appreciate the intricacies of this emotion in a way no classroom ever could. You taught us to explore and appreciate the different aspects of this spellbinding moments that go beyond simple explanations.

You have shown me that love is not just a word or a fleeting feeling; it is a deep and multifaceted experience. I learned from you that love involves understanding, patience, and commitment. You offer me a way to connect with my emotions and navigate my relationships with a better understanding.

You showed me that love is not always about presence, it is about connection. Probably, that is the reason we have not met, yet I love you and feel a bond with you in a way that is above any definition. Shah Rukh, if I know what it is to love without limits and if I know how to love unconditionally and wholeheartedly, it is because of you, and for that, I will always be indebted.

Love You.

Priyanka

Home Makeover Story

Dear Shah Rukh,

I wanted to ask you something. You have been making films for a long time. Has it ever happened to you that you watch a movie, your own or otherwise, and it changed your life? It inspired, motivated, and excited you, urging you to take action. It touched your heart, changed your thoughts, or offered a fresh perspective on life. One that filled you with new ideas and left you feeling eager to embrace challenges.

People tell me some films are not just entertainment; they are catalysts for growth and change, leaving a lasting impact on your mind and spirit. They are the stories that stay with you long after the credits roll, shaping your outlook and inspiring your journey.

Has it ever happened to you, Shah Rukh? Though I am not a big movie enthusiast yet, your movies have such an effect on me. They are not just entertainment. I laugh, I cry, feel warm and get angry while watching your movies. They give me a glimpse into the latest fashion trends and styles. Even when I am out of the theatre, their spell does not easily fade. While I return to reality, a part of the characters you portray on screen still lingers in my thoughts. The escapism they provide is not just a momentary break from everyday chaos, it stays with me for quite some time.

Although Shah Rukh, as much as I want to watch your movies simply as entertainment and to pass the time, they stir my emotions, inspire me to go get the things I want in life, not be afraid to pursue my dreams and face all the challenges head-on. They have moved me in a way that changed my life for good. Today, I want to talk about one of your movies that is not only close to my heart but also brought a dreamlike transformation into my home, turning it upside down. It was *Devdas!!!*

When *Devdas* hit the screens, my aunt, the one who first introduced me to you, was utterly captivated. Her excitement about the movie was clear from her body language and the way she spoke. She started wearing a bigger and bolder red *bindi* on her forehead. Her hairstyle was inspired by the looks of Aishwarya Ma'am and in her day-to-day conversation, she started using phrases and dialogues from the movie.

She could not stop talking to my mom about you and the movie. In an Indian middle-class family, where the *Nanad-Bhabhi* relationship is hyped to be bitter, my mom and my aunt shared a cordial bond. They spoke for hours over call, discussed new recipes, scrutinized common relatives, and explored the latest saree collection together. May God protect their bond from evil eyes.

"You must see Devdas, bhabhi," she would insist. "And watch it in the theatre."

"Shah Rukh's performance is more than extraordinary, bhabhi. There is so much depth and intensity you would feel while watching him. His eyes are so expressive. They would make you feel the ecstasy of true love and convey the despair of heartbreak. The guilt of indecision and the depths of self-destruction, his eyes convey them all. You don't need a spoken word when you can express all your emotions through your eyes. I am telling you, the moment you see tears in his eyes, you will not be able to stop yours as well."

"And Aishwarya and Madhuri," she continued, "They were gorgeous. Aishwarya's dignity, grace, and strength were admirable. Madhuri's elegance and wisdom will also leave you spellbound."

She hardly took a pause and went on, "The sets, bhabhi, they were palatial! There were rich cultural backdrops and lavish costumes. The movie is a must-watch in a theatre."

"And the songs!", she sighed as she rested her left hand on her chest, tilting her head to the side. Her eyes closed in admiration and her lips stretched, forming a pleasant curve. "The beats, the lyrics, the music and the dance performances, they are breath-taking," she was nonstop.

She went on for an hour painting a vivid picture of the movie, the songs, the sets, and the entire cast, describing their charm and beauty. As for the way she tried to sell *Devdas* to us, I can assure you, Shah Rukh, she will be an excellent addition to your PR and marketing teams.

The way my aunt had tried to pitch in *Devdas* intrigued my mom and I just wished she kept talking about you. Her enthusiasm for the film was contagious. Although Mom was curious to watch the movie but held her emotions in check. One reason was that the movie outings were reserved for special occasions in our family and the second, she considered engaging in such leisure as a waste of money. However, this time, her curious self was taking over her usual restraint. Taking advantage of the situation, I played my card.

"Mom, please, let's go watch it. Everyone says Devdas is a great movie. You already heard the buzz around Shah Rukh's performance and the film's grandeur. How could you ignore this one?" I looked at her with a pleading expression, hoping to get what I wanted.

The puppy eyes worked. After a little more persuasion, she finally relented, and we were all eager to experience the enchantment of *Devdas* together.

When my mother expressed her desire to watch the movie with my father, he agreed wholeheartedly. He promised he would take us to see the movie soon. But like I said, we could not go to the movies much for a few reasons. Nevertheless, my dad would do everything in his capacity to make my mom happy.

My dad is a wonderfully cheerful and forgetful man. His ability to forget things in the blink of an eye is quite remarkable. He might forget our birthdays. He could forget he had given someone time to meet and could even forget he had to pick us up from school. Perhaps, the key to his happiness also lies in the fact that he would easily overlook past grievances, dismiss unkind words, and forget even the most recent family arguments or the last ugly conversation he had with his siblings. "Delete Unnecessary Data" is the mantra of his cheerfulness and lightheartedness. However, when he forgot he went to the local dairy shop with Fufa Ji, promising him a ride of the neighbourhood, but returned all by himself, it was a bit of a nuisance!

But there is one thing he would never forget—what Mom asks or tells him. Despite his tendency to forget almost everything else, he always remembers her requests and instructions. It is as if his mind has a special compartment reserved for her. So, I was certain, knowing my mom's wishes, he would take us out to see the movie for sure. But he had something else planned for us.

The next day, he made a special effort for us to watch Devdas by renting a cassette. A cassette! Can you imagine Shah Rukh? We watched Devdas on a dubbed cassette! Those were the days when VCRs were a rage. We used to watch a lot of movies on VCR. But having heard so much about you in *Devdas*, I felt let down. I had hoped to see you at the cinema. I wanted to experience the warmth, the depth, and the intensity you portrayed on the big screen. But all my dreams were shattered when Dad announced we would watch *Devdas* at home today. I doubted whether he referred to the movie or me!

Despite our initial argument regarding why he got the cassette and why we could not go to the movies, we gathered around to watch the movie together. My mom still appreciated and believed it was thoughtful of Dad to set up a movie night at home. However, as soon as we hit play, the reality of our situation became apparent. The quality of the cassette was far from what we had hoped for. The picture was grainy, and the colours were off, making it hard to distinguish the finer details of the scenes. To make matters worse, since it was a dubbed version, the audio was out of sync and the dialogue was often unclear. The technical shortcomings left me feeling disheartened and annoyed. It was nothing of the sort I had imagined.

Once the movie ended, Dad, ever the optimist, turned to Mom with a hopeful expression and asked if she enjoyed the film. Honestly, I thought, how could he even ask this question? Was it not apparent? Nonetheless, his tone was light, clearly trying to find a silver lining despite the less-than-ideal viewing conditions.

"Absolutely. I loved it". I was taken aback when my mom uttered these words.

"But," she continued diplomatically, giving a subtle hint of disappointment, "It would have been better if it was clearer. Watching it in the theatre would have its charm."

Her words were gentle, but there was an unmistakable undercurrent of dissatisfaction. She acknowledged the effort Dad had put into arranging the movie night but could not help but express that the experience would have been much more enjoyable if the quality had been better. She fondly reminisced about the unique charm of watching movies in a theatre, where the grandeur and clarity of the screen add a special touch to the experience.

I still remember my father's expression vividly. It was like he had failed an exam where he had expected to excel. His face wore a look of dismay and disappointment, a contrast to the usual confidence and cheerfulness he exuded. It was as though he had built up grand expectations, only to see them crumble before his eyes.

Persistence runs in our blood, Shah Rukh. When my dad saw the hint of dissatisfaction on my mother's face, he decided to make up for it. Although he is not good at giving surprises, most of them tend to be shocks instead, this time it was a pleasant surprise for us. Two days later, while returning from the office, he got us a CD/DVD player.

"Today we will watch Devdas on this, " he boasted, hoping to see my mom smile.

Instead, my mother responded, "That is fine, but where is the space to keep it?" she rolled her eyes, pointing at the old wooden table where our TV was placed, clearly concerned about where the new player would fit.

My mother, an art lecturer, has a deep appreciation for aesthetics and order. Her love for painting extended beyond her work; she saw beauty in every corner of our home and always sought to create harmony and elegance. Her practical approach is balanced with a refined sense of artistry, and she finds joy in making her surroundings both functional and beautiful.

The next day, determined to fulfil my mother's wishes, my father bought a new TV stand and replaced the old table with it. This stand was designed to hold both the TV and the new DVD player he had purchased, along with a compartment to store the CDs/DVDs. He also bought the Devdas DVD, and we spent that evening watching the movie again.

My mother was mesmerized by Aishwarya's attire, jewellery, looks and beautiful backgrounds, and you again captivated me.

"Did you like the movie?", my dad asked again. This time, confidence eluded his face and voice. He was sure to have made an impression on her beloved better half.

"Yes, it was so beautiful." The happiness on my mother's face was noticeably clear.

"Thank You," she said with a sense of satisfaction.

A crescent formed on my father's face.

She continued, "The clothes, jewellery, and the entire set were beautiful. And…" her face brightened up.

"And the songs! They were amazing," she said with a sense of urgency. "I bet seeing them in the movie hall would have been a whole unique experience with the music resonating through the theatre."

My mother utterly enjoyed the movie. She had been humming the songs of the movie continuously. As for me, for days later, I could not help but wonder what it would be like if it were me instead of Aishwarya or Madhuri. I mean, how incredible it would have been if it were me on the swings holding hands with you. Isshhh! Okay, I know, Shah Rukh, you fear swings, but I promise I will not let go of your hand. I will hold you tight. Always!

And your eyes... Oh My God!!! They intoxicate me. Every time a tear rolls down your cheeks, my heart aches. You have so deep and expressive eyes. They speak volumes, revealing the depths of your emotions without uttering a single word. It is as if they hold thousands of untold stories, and every time someone dares to look closer, they discover a new tale waiting to be told. They shine with a light that warms the world and makes it feel a little more alive.

Okay, Shah Rukh, as much as I want to get drowned in your eyes, let us get back to what was unfolding at my home. The story did not end there.

A few days later, we got yet another surprise. A sweet one. My dad bought two speakers, the big ones.

"Today we will watch Devdas with these speakers," he said excitedly. "It will feel like we are in a cinema hall," he hoped to impress my mom. "We will drop the curtains, dim the lights, full volume and..."

"Where will we put them?" Mom trailed him off, raising her brow, placing her right hand on her waist, and shaking her head in disapproval. She focused on practicalities over the surprise. In her meticulous nature, the new speakers were just another item to find a place for.

Eventually, Dad had a new showcase designed to hold the speakers. It took a week to get the work done. In our tiny home it was a grand display unit, much inspired by your movie. And finally, we watched Devdas for the fifth time on TV. We drew the curtains on and switched off the lights. With speakers, every dialogue echoed in the room, every song came to life. This time, it did feel like we were in a cinema hall.

"*Itne me to hall me hi dekh aate picture.*" My brother teased my dad.

While my father was trying to fulfil the family's desire, I could see the love in action between Mom and Dad.

And as you once said, Shah Rukh, '*love is in small things, and as long as you are there for each other and make each other laugh a bit, that is love*'.

I was witnessing the love between my parents firsthand. It was not about the movie but about the effort my dad put in to make us happy, and the understanding my mom showed. It was about their small gestures of love and care that spoke volumes about their relationship. I realized love is not just about grand gestures; it is about the little things we do for each other every day, very much in line with your idea of love.

From the VCR cassettes to the DVD player, the TV stand, the speakers and the showcase, you became the reason for remodelling our home. To this day, the showcase adds to the beauty of our home and holds the memories of that day. Mom decorated it with all our childhood toys, which till then she kept securely in a box. Those speakers with the DVD player still lie in one section of the showcase.

It is not just a piece of furniture for us, Shah Rukh. It is a repository of laughter, shared moments, and the enduring magic of *The Shah Rukh Khan*. In a way, it symbolizes the countless stories we have lived within the walls of our home. Every time I walk past the showcase, it rings a bell in my mind and the lines *Silsila ye Chahat ka...* start playing in my head, reminding me of those cherished memories.

So yes, your movies not only inspire me to make life-changing decisions but also remind me of the simple joys and meaningful moments that shape our lives. And when it is an SRK movie, they offer a lens through which I see the love and laughter that shape my world. They remind me of the warmth and wonder that fills our lives. Shah Rukh, you have been an eternal part of our lives. Your charm always goes beyond the screen, sometimes leaving an everlasting impression on our hearts and sometimes being a reason for a change bringing happiness. And for me, that charm once turned four plain walls into a space where dreams, admiration, and love lived side by side.

Love you.

Priyanka

Ekta's Aman

Dear Shah Rukh,

In my earlier letters, I introduced you to the two ladies in my family who deeply admire you. Today, I want you to meet the third special one. I call her '*Chota Jasoos, Small Wonder, Bandariya, Pagaliya*' and what not. Her name is Ekta. She is my sister and is twelve years younger than me.

Ekta is someone who knows everything about me, the one I can trust with all my secrets, and she is always the first to share any news about our family happenings with me. She knows everything about everyone. She is full of life and brings a lot of joy wherever she goes.

One of Ekta's special talents is her ability to make people smile. She is good at imitating people and situations, especially scenes from movies. It is amazing how she can mimic someone's voice or actions and make it seem so real! Just being around her can lift anyone's spirits.

To me, she is not just a little sister; she is a daughter too and I am very protective of her. She is also a friend I can laugh with and share my thoughts with.

I wanted you to know about her because she is one of the crazy women in our family who loves you beyond words can describe.

Growing up, they said, *Choti behan k chattis k chattis guund badi behan k sikhaye huye hote hai*. Well, I cannot agree more. I have taught her a lot of things, including her very first action song, *Tum pas aye*, when she was four years old. I introduced you to her at a very early age and she started liking you instantly.

We grew up together watching all your movies like *Kuch Kuch Hota Hai, Phir Bhi Dil hai Hindustani, Josh* and so on. The song, *Apun Bola* from *Josh*, used to be her favourite and *I am the best* her favourite tagline. When she sang the lyrics in her childish, not-so-clear tone, we could not stop laughing and loving her.

Then came your *Kal Ho Na Ho*—a movie that cast the same spell on her that Deewana cast on me. We loved the movie. But mostly, we loved Aman. We loved everything about Aman. His style, his sense of humour, his compassion, everything.

Ekta was the same age as the little girl, Jia, in the movie and used to refer to you as Mera Aman. We would fight over you, "He is mine!!" While I hugged your posters, she would pose like you in every photo taken. While I would write poems, lost in your thoughts, she would recite those poems, imagining you were in front of her. Good Old days!

She would try to mimic your iconic dialogues, copy your dance steps and fake cry, enacting you. Like I had a collection of your pictures in my notebook, she had your posters in every corner of her room. She compiled a list of all your iconic dialogues and recited those with a different emotional touch.

For example, she would deliver your romantic dialogue while laughing like an idiot. She would say an intense or angry dialogue as if she were in a freezing temperature. Some of your funniest dialogues were delivered in a manner as if she was dead scared. It was funny.

She would spend hours making fun of your dialogues herself, but the moment anyone else tried to do that, she would get her back up. She becomes defensive and is ready to hunt them down. I think she is more outgoing in showing off her feelings for you, unlike me, who keeps them to my heart.

When I moved out of home for my studies, she was only eight. She would write me letters. After filling me in about what was happening at home and her school, she would write about you at length. Which movie she watched recently, what she liked about you, how cute you looked and how perfectly you danced. She would scribble several pages, writing just about you.

As we grew up, our bond with you and with each other grew stronger. Once, when I got a text from her which read, "I met Shah Rukh", hundreds of thoughts crossed my mind simultaneously.

"What? "

"Really?"

"You are kidding me?"

"Did she lose her phone? "

"Is this a message from an imposter? "

"This must be another one of her pranks!"

I could not contain my excitement for more than a minute. I dialled her. "Where are you? I got a text, is that true...", while I went on bombarding her with questions in excitement, I could hear her sob, and all my excitement went down the drain. My thoughts instantly shifted to her well-being.

"Hey, what happened? Are you all right?" I was concerned about her.

"I saw him," her voice was shaking. "Just a few feet away from me."

"It was surreal. I wanted to touch him, speak to him, but just could not move." I could sense the vulnerability in her voice.

Shah Rukh, like you, she is an alumnus of Delhi University. By virtue of being a student of DU, she got an opportunity to see you in person. It was an event at Hans Raj College, where you came for a while.

All she told me was, "Didi, I froze in time. Tears kept flowing and among all the hooting and noise around, I could only hear one voice. Everything else had faded away." She then went on to describe the effect your presence had on her. It was divine.

What a lucky girl! I mean, I have not got this chance yet. I feel a little jealous of her.

Two years ago, she got married. As we geared up for her wedding, we also prepared for her sangeet ceremony. She requested me to prepare a dance performance for the event. As if she had to. I mean, how could I not be dancing on such a beautiful occasion? I had a huge wish list for her wedding. Seeing her in a bride's abode was one of my most cherished dreams.

On her big day, she performed first, and my dance number followed it. When both our performances were over, my brother came over and whispered to us, " You two just can't get over Shah Rukh, can you?".

We looked at each other, confused, and then looked at my brother. He made a silly face. The one he always makes while teasing us about you. It was then we realized that all the songs that we had selected for our dance performance were from your movies. From *Mehandi Laga k Rakhna* to *Mahi Ve* and from *Bholi si Surat* to *Tujhme Rab Dikhta Hai* every single song we both performed was performed by you first.

As the realization sank in, the three of us smiled at each other. Ekta turned to my brother, "It's not just the two of us—our whole family is never getting over Shah Rukh!", she smirked.

She pointed a finger at the stage where our entire clan had collected to dance to the tunes of *Khai Ke Paan Banaras Wala* from your Don, especially the Fufa Ji's. At one point I just stood at the corner of the hall observing the smiling faces and the people swaying with the music. It was a beautiful and fun-filled evening where a four-year-old enjoyed it as much as an eighty-year-old did.

Shah Rukh, none of us could imagine a day of happiness without your presence in some or the other form. Our special days become extra special because of you. When anyone tells me and Ekta are your biggest fans, it feels annoying and insulting. The feeling we harbour for you is way beyond the admiration of a fan. It is more like an unwavering, unconditional, and divine love.

Forget it, Shah Rukh! The more I try, the more I fail. I cannot describe to you, or anyone else, how we both feel about you. Huh!

Anyway, as time passed, we found ourselves separated by the demands of marriage, jobs, and other life situations. However, amidst these changes, you, Shah Rukh, remained the thread that bound us together. The memories associated with you have been a constant source of happiness and connection for both Ekta and me.

Every time your new movie hits the screen, you win an award, host a show or even when you run into controversy, it ignites a deep conversation between me and Ekta. It feels like someone of our own is going through that phase. We feel happy and take pride in your achievements. It saddens us when people wrong you. We feel frustrated and angry when you are in trouble.

In conclusion, Shah Rukh, you are a constant companion for both of us. You are a source of joy, laughter, and shared memories that continue to strengthen the bond between my little sister, Ekta, and me. Your influence has enriched our lives in ways that words cannot fully express.

We believe we are connected to you in some way. How else can you care for someone so sincerely? Feel happy in someone else's happiness, sad in someone else's sadness and pray for someone's wellbeing in challenging times. I pray to God this connection that we believe we have with you prevails forever.

Love You

Priyanka

A Ghostly Affair

Dear Shah Rukh,

College time is the best time of our lives. Isn't it? We are old enough to have independence and make our own choices, yet young enough to explore and embrace new experiences without the full weight of responsibilities. College life is filled with so many memorable experiences. Late-night study sessions, campus events, parties, sports, games, and volunteering opportunities are to name a few. Then there are friends we make for a lifetime. The shared experiences, challenges and adventures with friends are invaluable and often form the foundation of lifelong bonds and cherished memories.

I am sure you would have a few incidents during your college days that you look back on and tell your kids. That one close friend, or that strangest teacher, or your favorite prank, or your most kinky and flirtatious attitude, there must be something that you miss about your college.

Well, I had a very enjoyable college life and want to share with you a brief incident.

It was between 2004 and 2008. I studied in Greater Noida. Back then, it was a complete jungle, a completely deserted land. It was a place where even something as simple as buying a piece of stationery meant taking a trip to another city.

During those times, we had to walk two kilometres from the campus hostel to get a rickshaw to the nearest bus stop. Whether it was rushing to stock up on Maggie noodles for our midnight cravings or celebrating each other's birthdays, we would make the long journey to Delhi and back, always keeping a close eye on the hostel's timeline. Semester exams felt even more challenging during the scorching summer heat or the chilling winter breeze, adding an extra layer of drama to the already stressful times.

"I don't know how she will survive there; it is such a deserted area", were my father's words to my mom when he left me at the hostel and returned home.

Most of us stayed in hostels and had stepped out of their homes for the very first time. We were scared, yet excited about the new life to unfold. Sometimes we would feel homesick and yet other times we were ready to rock and roll. With a limited number of people having access to mobile phones, during the first year of our college, it was difficult to stay connected to our families. So, we made our new world. The classmates, hostel mates, teachers, wardens, deans and even the peons and maids were all part of our new world.

Bunking the classes, going on strike just before the mid-semester exams and exploding the chemistry lab with awful experiments, we did it all. It was fun. We had nicknames for each other. Pogo, Ghanti, Chuza, Chilgoza, and Chammach were a few of them.

In that small world of ours, we were unaware of what was happening on other parts of the earth. Our focus was on navigating through our daily routines and making the most of the moments we shared. Despite the difficulties, the friendship, the mutual trust, and the shared experiences made our time in Greater Noida memorable and special. It was a time of simplicity and closeness, where the bonds we forged with each other became the centre of our universe.

Life was challenging during those four years, but the friends we made there made it enjoyable. We relied on each other for support and laughter, teasing one another and offering encouragement whenever needed. The constant leg-pulling and cheering each other during tough times were the way of life there. Sometimes those playful banters started amidst an ongoing class and were aimed at irritating and annoying the teacher. At other times, it was targeted at a single person and the entire class would gang against them.

Once I was the target for such a leg-pulling session in the classroom. Shah Rukh, I am a quiet, shy and introvert girl. I may not be the first one to go on and strike up a conversation with the next person in the room, but if someone starts a conversation, they are sure to find a pleasant company. I was (and I am) a friend to everyone in the class and a very easy target for the group roasting session.

One day, after our first lecture was over and the teacher for the second lecture had not yet come in, a friend started, "Priyanka, would you like to date a Ghost?".

Taken by surprise, it took me a few seconds to understand what he was referring to and when I understood what he was talking about, I gave back an annoying look.

"Yeah, how would a candlelight dinner with a ghost feel like?" another one jumped in with a mischievous grin, "Ghostly! Isn't it?" while pulling a crooked, grumpy face for dramatic effect.

"How would a ghost ask you out—Would you be my dinner tonight?" poked a third one, his voice dripping with playful sarcasm as he raised an eyebrow.

It did not take me much time to understand it would not be an easy way out of this group ragging session. Everyone in the classroom had ganged up on me and took turns pulling my leg with all sorts of hilarious antics!

Shah Rukh, I am not sure how this happens, but everyone around me knows my fondness for you. Be it family or friends, classmates, or colleagues or, for that matter, even my hairdresser, one way or the other, they know my fascination about you. No matter how much I try to keep it low-key, somehow, it gets out there. It seems my admiration for you has a way of speaking for itself, louder than I ever intended. And once they know, they never miss a chance to tease me about it, turning my admiration into a favourite topic for playful banter.

That day, as the leg-pulling session went on longer than usual, it felt like the entire class knew about my admiration for you and everyone started teasing me while pointing to your character in *Paheli*.

For a while, I tried to laugh off and remain silent. But then I joined in the fun.

"Why? Are you guys jealous?", I gave a mischievous look, raising an eyebrow with a playful smirk.

"Oh, I see," I said, tilting my head with a sly grin, my eyes gleaming with mischief, "You don't get anyone to date you even when you are alive, while he is scoring dates even as a ghost," finishing with a mock pout and a playful wink.

Another one chipped in, "Yeah, who does not like a ghost to snuggle her. I am sure Priyanka will not mind cuddling with a ghost," wagging their eyebrows playfully and giving a mock shiver as if imagining it.

"Why not?" I said with a wicked smile, leaning in conspiratorially. "If it's Shah Rukh, it is pure, supernatural love—you can't beat that!" I added with a dramatic flourish, pointing my fingers at the guys in the room as if to challenge them to top that.

"Oh! She is saying her perfect man is a ghost," one of them declared to the rest of the class.

"No! I am saying a perfect man is nothing but an illusion," I corrected him with a sly grin. "And I am happy if that illusion for me is Shah Rukh. Even as an illusion, Shah Rukh embodies my idea of perfection." I tried to wrap up the conversation decisively, much like a judge delivering a final verdict on a contentious case.

It went on for a while. The entire class kept cracking jokes about me and the illusory Shah Rukh Khan, but I fired back each time, insisting that you, Shah Rukh, are the best. You are the epitome of perfection, a standard no one else could ever match up to—of course, it is out of jealousy and insecurity that they are making those comments!

Amidst this laughter, we did not realize when the teacher came in until he screamed, "Class, what is going on?".

"Priyanka is having a ghostly affair," came a prompt reply from the back bench.

The class burst into laughter while I was looking for a place to hide from the teacher's gaze. Confused, the teacher looked at me. I was fidgeting with my fingers, my cheeks turning slightly pink as I avoided eye contact, nervously shifting in my seat.

"She has the ability to embrace the supernatural powers," shouted another, making me blush even deeper, my hands awkwardly gripping the edges of my desk as I sank lower into my seat, hoping the ground would swallow me up.

The teacher hushed the class after a few more remarks.

"What is going on, Priyanka? I can't imagine a girl like you having an affair. Focus on your studies, beta," said the teacher with utmost concern on his face. It was as if one of his family members had strayed and he wanted them back on the right path.

"Sir, when the ghost is this charming, loving him is absolutely inevitable," I replied sheepishly, my voice trailing off as I nervously shuffled in my seat, avoiding the teacher's gaze, not realizing that he was still completely unaware of the context.

"What ghost?" asked the teacher, now annoyed more than ever.

"Shah Rukh Khan," came a screeching reply. The class burst into laughter, and I felt my face turn bright red, shrinking into my seat, desperately wishing I could disappear as the giggles echoed around the room.

The teacher, now intrigued by the ongoing banter, asked one of us to explain what was going on. When he grasped the context, he let out a sigh, shaking his head side to side, and with a mischievous smile, joined in the fun, becoming part of the leg-pulling session all aimed at me.

My face flushed when the teacher, too, joined in. I could only manage to display a shy smile, but inside, my mind was far from the classroom. It had drifted somewhere else—somewhere where only you and I existed, Shah Rukh. As the laughter settled and the class resumed, the world around me became a distant hum, fading into the background like a scene transitioning into soft focus in one of your romantic montages. My mind was completely consumed by your thoughts, your charm, your wit, and your effortless ability to make every moment surreal.

And then, a whimsical thought crept into my mind, one I could not shake no matter how hard I tried. I could not help but wonder, if not in this life, what would it be like dating you as a ghost? The idea made me smile, a sweet, secret smile. It was ridiculous, surreal, and yet, in its own way, a perfectly fitting dream for the kind of love you represent, timeless, boundless, and utterly enchanting.

My thoughts were abruptly interrupted when a piece of chalk came flying toward my face.

"Lachchi, pay attention," said the teacher with a playful smile, clearly enjoying my distraction.

The class roared with laughter, and for the next four years, I got a new nickname.

The day continued as usual, but my heart remained elsewhere, caught in a delightful daydream that only you, Shah Rukh, could inspire. The teasing had long subsided, and yet, a quiet smile lingered on my face, like a secret only I understood.

My thoughts wandered to the ridiculous, yet enchanting idea of sharing a realm beyond the ordinary with you. The idea was absurd, yet in its own way, strangely fitting. After all, love, real love, defies logic, boundaries, even lifetimes.

The bell rang, jolting me back to the present, but the warmth of the moment stayed with me. As I packed my books and stepped out of the classroom, a deep realization dawned upon me: while the world may tease, question, or laugh at my devotion, it does not matter. My admiration for you, Shah Rukh, is mine alone, a little piece of magic in an otherwise ordinary world. And whether it is on this plane or beyond, that magic, that connection, will always feel real to me.

Love You,

Priyanka

Mom Vs Me

Dear Shah Rukh,

"Na Apno se Khulta hai,

Na Gairo se Khulta hai,

Ye Jannat ka Darwaza Hai

Ye Meri Maa ke Pairo se Khulta hai"

You must have heard these quotes. Beautiful lines. Though I do not know the source, the verse beautifully highlights the idea that some of the most profound and sacred experiences and blessings in life are directly connected to a mother's love and presence. It reflects the sincere respect and reverence for the mother figure, portraying her as a gateway to heavenly experiences. So true.

We all love our mothers. Moms are our friends, philosophers, and guides. They are our go-to person for all the problems. They have a solution for almost everything. I call mine Mrs. Fix-it Fairy.

Mothers hold a special place in our hearts. They are selfless. They love us unconditionally, are protective of us, and are always ready to help and guide us through life. Their support is like a firm foundation, shaping us into the individuals we are meant to be. They play a huge role in our lives. No matter what mistake we make, they will always be by our side. In sickness, their gentle touch will make us feel better and after a long and tiring day, nothing compares to the warmth of a mother's hug. The bond with our mothers is truly special and important. No one can love you and understand you more than a mom.

Now, before I say one more sentence, I want to be completely honest; I love my mom very much. Having said that, there is another truth about Mums. Mothers can be finicky sometimes. They are fussy, hard to please, perfectionist and over-critical. Mine, in particular, is extra finicky, and I suspect even my relatives and neighbours might be wary of her. Do not get me wrong, she is not irritable or tyrannical. It is just that she is incredibly straightforward and blunt. She does not keep things to herself; she says them out loud, and as you might imagine, dealing with such honesty can be challenging.

I rarely argue with her, after all, she is my gateway to heaven. But when we clash, it is like diving headfirst into a personal hell. Her sarcastic quips and teasing comments are like being caught in a storm of insults that is impossible to escape. And to make it worse, every word she says is a bitter truth. So, to keep my pass to heaven open, I try my best not to push her buttons, all the while admiring that her no-nonsense attitude is part of what makes her so wonderfully unique. In a nutshell, she is a typical Indian mom.

Despite my best efforts to keep her happy, there are moments when my attempts fall short. At first, she will be quietly ignoring everything as if it was some meaningless nonsense not worthy of her time and attention. But, Oh My God! If her patience dies, we are in soup.

On those lines, I have a small story for you, Shah Rukh! This incident occurred during the release of your film, *Don*.

Your arrival as *Don* felt like falling in love with you all over again, but this time with a fire I could not ignore. You were devastatingly sensuous, a sight that made the world around you fade away. In that sleek black suit, you were a masterpiece of elegance and raw power. Every detail pulled me closer to your magnetic charm.

It was strange; I started thinking that smoking makes you look irresistibly hot. Though I do not smoke myself, nor do I endorse it. But you, you looked undeniably attractive. The cigarette slid between your fingers with effortless ease, each movement drawing my eyes like a moth to a flame. The way you brought it to your lips, slow and deliberate, sent a thrill through me that I could not shake. An irresistible air of mystery was added by the way smoke swirled around your face. Oh, I so badly wished I was a cigarette.

Your smirk, full of confidence and just a touch of wickedness, made my heart race, while your intense eyes seemed to hold me in place, daring me to look away. Every glance, every subtle motion, felt like a spell cast just for me. You did not just enter the screen; you owned it, and in doing so, you owned me too. It was as if you wielded a sophisticated and alluring charm that swept me off my feet, leaving me spellbound in your captivating presence.

Oh! I can feel my heart throbbing hard in my chest as I pen down your looks from Don!

Your portrayal of Don was hypnotic, to say the least. It was as if you had cast a spell, leaving me and everyone else captivated by your charisma. What added to the enchantment was the song *Khaike Paan Banaras Wala*. Yeah, one reason it was (and is) special to us is that we are all from Banaras. Whenever the song played, it was as if the entire city could not resist dancing to its tunes.

However, whenever the song played, there was one person who was not happy. Guess who? Yes, my mom. She would always raise her brow and twist her face, saying, "Play the original. This one is just a copy," referring to Amit Ji's version of the song.

My mom did not take to you at all, though she was a devoted fan of Mr. Amitabh Bachchan. She dismissively used to call you a copycat. I have to admit, Shah Rukh, it was frustrating for me to hear that, especially when I admired you so much. But everyone has their tastes, right? We cannot compel people to love something, even if we think they are missing something extraordinary. My mom, well, has always been a little finicky, opinionated, and very set in her ways. That is who she is, and I learned to let her opinions roll off my back. After all, love for someone is personal, and hers simply belonged to another era.

Anyway, she was not as obsessed with Amit Ji as I was, (and I am) with you, but her admiration for Mr. Bachchan was undeniable. Everyone in my family admired him. This admiration for Mr. Bachchan reached its peak during the days of Kaun Banega Crorepati (KBC).

KBC became a cherished tradition in our family. It was a time when all five of us would gather around the television, eagerly awaiting the next episode. Each member of our family found something different to appreciate in the show.

For my mother, it was the sheer presence of Mr. Bachchan himself, whom she held in such high esteem. His charisma and intellect left her in awe every time he appeared on screen.

My father, on the other hand, was happy with KBC, as it gave him a break from the melodramatic daily soaps my mother would make him watch every day.

As for my brother and I, we found KBC to be both entertaining and educational. We loved trying to answer the questions, along with the contestants.

And then there was my little sister, who was simply thrilled to be allowed to watch TV with the rest of us.

That one hour of TV time was something each of us would look forward to. Mom would wrap up dinner before showtime. We would finish our homework and gather around in the dining room. We would sit together, make bets on the questions, and pass comments on the contestants. It was our family's happy time.

But You, are you! You will not stop. It seemed like the peace and happiness levels of my family were off the charts for you! You know how it is when you are excited about something, but not everyone shares your enthusiasm? That is exactly how it was in our house when you, Mr. Khan, went from being the charming Don to hosting Kaun Banega Crorepati.

It was like a whirlwind of emotions swirling around our family TV time. I was over the moon when I heard you were going to be the KBC host. To me, it meant I could see you every day. What more can a love-stricken person ask for than meeting the love of her life every single day? But here is the twist: while I was dancing on clouds, my mom was more like a storm brewing. She was not exactly thrilled about your hosting KBC. Nope, not at all.

It was during one of the semester's breaks that I returned from college when we had a casual conversation about the new host on KBC. I tried to tease her playfully about you replacing Big B. but I got a vibe from her that said, "Don't you bring that up again". I could completely feel the disappointment in my mother's tone when she spoke about the show and hence did not take that conversation any further.

Still, despite her reservations, we all gathered around the TV each evening to watch KBC together. For me, it felt the time had stopped. It took an eternity for the clock to strike nine. Every day I waited eagerly for you to show up, right in our living room. And as the show started, I would start a conversation with you in my mind. It was naïve of me, I knew, but what else could I do? Meeting you in person was a far-fetched dream.

But for my mom, it was a different story altogether. She was not so happy because she could not see her favourite person, Mr. Amitabh Bachchan, as much as she used to. To her, Amitabh Ji was the real deal. He was the original Don, the original KBC host, and she was not about to let anyone forget it.

One evening, as the show ended, I was gushing about how cute and talented you were to my siblings, and how your anchoring made us laugh our lungs out, and how each episode was more fun than ever. Ekta and Varun both agreed with me. Me and Ekta are always on your side, but it surprised me when Varun expressed his genuine admiration for you. And when dad joined in, mom could not hold back her anymore.

Amidst the laughter and admiration for you came a screeching voice, "Cute? Talented?", a very familiar tone that had an underlying meaning: "That's it. Don't you dare utter another word appreciating him".

"Really! Cute?" she repeated. I could see the wrinkles form on her forehead while her eyes shrank.

.

"He is just a copycat!" came another sharp retort.

I exchanged a puzzled look with Ekta and Varun, unable to understand what went wrong. I opened my mouth and before I could utter a word, she started again as her index finger pointed towards me.

"All he does is mimic Amitabh Bachchan. Amitabh Ji did Don, so he had to do Don. Amitabh Ji started KBC, so here he is, following in his footsteps. What does he want to prove?" her pointed finger swayed from me to the television and back in the air.

My mouth remained open, my eyes widened, and my senses lost. My mind could not process what was happening.

"Mom, why are you being mean?" Ekta said, holding Mom's hand trying to calm her down. She pulled her hand back with a jerk.

"Earlier he tried copying Dilip Kumar Ji in Devdas, now he is trying to imitate Amit Ji. Does your Shah Rukh have an originality of his own?", she continued as her gaze shifted from me to the other two siblings.

She was fuming. Her face twisted as she gave an annoying look. We could feel the tension in the air.

For a moment, it felt like the room was frozen. It was a pin-drop silence for the next few seconds when my dad broke it.

"Yes, you're right. What does he even know about acting!" Dad tried to calm her down.

He agreed with her, trying to ease the tension. I gave my Dad a surprising look, to which he responded with a wink, showing he was still on my side.

I looked at Varun giving an expression asking for his support on the matter. He blinked his eyes in assurance and just when I thought I had an ally, my brother decided to join the fun.

He fueled the fire. "Mom is right, you know," I could imagine his face turning into the devil smiley that we have on WhatsApp now.

"One, your Shah Rukh looks like a chipmunk," he continued, "Second, to earn a living he must do something, so he copies everyone. The easiest way to make money is to mimic. Even I can do that," he gave the devil's grin.

It was like a united front surrounded me against my admiration for you. I could understand why Mom was upset. She often hides her genuine emotions behind weird comments. But I was still a little disappointed. I wanted her to see the charm and charisma that I saw in you, Shah Rukh. I wanted her to like the man I was so fond of, at least a little.

Well, that discussion continued for a while, with Mom, Dad, and my brother determined to send my blood pressure soaring. Every comment and counter-argument seemed designed to test my patience. My Mom's unwavering critique, my Dad's attempts to mediate, and my brother's teasing remarks all combined to create a perfect storm of frustration. Gradually, my mum cooled down and now they were all bullying me.

While they laughed and giggled, making fun of you, I could feel my heart racing and my head spinning as they each took turns pushing my buttons, leaving me exasperated and wondering if we would ever reach a consensus. I was all worked up and could bite someone's head off.

I took a deep breath. Collecting my thoughts, and with a firm conviction in my voice, I said, "Only Shah Rukh can pull off what Amit ji does. No one else has that kind of talent, trust me".

My pitch was higher than usual. For a moment, everybody paused. Ekta gave me a wide-eyed look as if saying, "Di, do not mess with Mom."

I could not stop, though. "And you spoke of Devdas, Mom." I turned to her, agitated. "Name one other actor who could have portrayed the character with ten per cent of perfection what Shah Rukh portrayed." My voice trailed off as I managed to hold my frustration.

"She also has a point", my father sided with me after a brief pause, sensing my vulnerability.

My sister chimed in, "I wonder if mom is upset with Shah Rukh because he is overshadowing Mr. Bachchan or because both of her daughters are in love with this man who is already married and is much older than they are," in her jovial teasing tone.

The room burst into laughter instantly with her hilarious tone and comment, and this debate went out throughout the night.

What started as a simple disagreement transformed into a full-fledged debate that continued throughout the night. The house echoed with arguments, laughter, and anecdotes about our favourite moments from your and Big B's movies and shows. What began as a source of annoyance transformed into an evening filled with lively discussions and shared memories.

In the end, the debate may not have led to a unanimous decision, but it brought us closer as a family. We understood each other's likes and dislikes. We learned to respect each other's choices. The night may have started with arguments, but it concluded with the warmth of familial bonds.

Amidst the countless debates about who is best, you, Shah Rukh, stand unrivalled in my heart. Your presence brings joy to our family gatherings, turning ordinary moments into cherished memories. Each time you grace our screens; you bring a unique joy that lingers in our memories long after the show ends. Here is to the love, laughter, and timeless debates you have ignited in our lives.

Love You,

Priyanka

Serendipity

Dear Shah Rukh,

Like you, I am a firm believer in hard work. I hold a strong faith in my heart that if you give one hundred per cent to your dreams, they will materialize in the way you deserve. I work towards meticulous planning and execution, always striving to control as much as I can. But you cannot control everything all the time. Sometimes everything slips your hand, and you cannot do much about it. All you can do is hold on for one more minute and then the magic happens.

There was an event in my life when despite putting in all my efforts, nothing seemed to be moving forward. I found myself in despair. And then, just when I was about to lose hope, an unexpected series of events turned in my favour. It felt like the universe had conspired to give me a helping hand. Serendipity!

It made me pause and wonder about the power of those random moments that can change everything. Do you believe in serendipity, Shah Rukh? Do you think there is a mysterious force that aligns things in our favour when we least expect it?

Well, I did not believe in the power of serendipity until a special episode occurred in my life. It changed my perspective and made me reconsider the idea of unexpected, fortunate moments. Sometimes, things happen in a way that we could not predict or plan, and this incident made me realize the beauty of such serendipitous occurrences.

It was August 2007; the fifth semester had begun. It was a crucial time for us as students. A time every engineering student awaits. Our hard work would pay off soon and the dreams of our parents would come true. Soon we would have job offers, we would be independent, responsible people and would be taken seriously in the family. All because our recruitment drive had started, and the placement opportunities were knocking on our doors. Many companies were conducting their recruitment drives, both on-campus and off-campus.

We were all geared up, ready to take the next leap in our lives. Every single student was busy polishing their skills. Some joined aptitude classes and some coding classes. A few took mock interview sessions and others personality development classes. The college conducted workshops and seminars providing technical and motivational guidance. From group study to preparing for mock interviews, the entire batch was focused on one thing: securing a job.

While my roommate, also my classmate, would often insist I take fun breaks and go to movies, I would rather prefer to do something more constructive and productive. Securing a job and having financial independence was the ultimate reason I opted for an engineering course far away from home. I did not want my parents to marry me to some NRI as soon as I completed my graduation just like any other girl in a middle-class family.

Getting married to someone and relying on him for my everyday needs was the most dreadful thought. I wanted to be independent and be able to take care of my ageing parents. I had dreamt of living in my own house and driving my own Hyundai i10. I wanted to take international vacations with family and wanted to face the world on my terms. Getting a decent placement was the very first step in realizing my dreams. It was nonnegotiable for me, something I could not compromise in any way.

Getting a job from a campus interview was not as easy as we thought. Sometimes we did not meet the eligibility criteria and other times there were several elimination rounds. At times the interview locations were far off and impossible to travel to, other times there were limited openings.

Amidst all these challenges, I was hopeful and kept going with my preparation. I had a clear goal and was working towards it diligently. Finally, I got my chance. One evening, my placement coordinator, also my classmate and friend called up to inform me that one Multinational Organization had scheduled its recruitment drive in a college in Ghaziabad the next day. He informed me I met the eligibility criteria and asked if I would be interested in travelling to Ghaziabad for this interview.

I felt a sudden rush of joy, merely at the thought of getting an opportunity. When I confirmed my willingness to attend the recruitment drive, he sent me the details regarding the process, number and types of interview rounds, documents required for the interview, dress code to put on, et cetera.

This was my first job interview. Excitement and nervousness bubbled in me. I had worked hard to prepare for the interview. I did not, or so did I believe, leave any stone unturned for this opportunity. The only challenge I felt was reaching the venue of this event on time as the college did not provide the conveyance.

I spent the evening going through the interview guidelines, and collecting all the required documents, including my resume, mark sheets, identity cards et cetera. I ironed a pair of formal dress and polished my shoes as bright as I could. I wanted to sleep early and be relaxed for the next day, but the excitement and nervousness did not let me.

Sleep was far from my eyes. I stood on the balcony of my room lost in anticipation of the coming morning humming the lines from your song, Shah Rukh: "*Aaj ki raat, hona hai kya, pana hai kya, khona hai kya*" when water sprinkled over me. It had started to drizzle. I smiled.

You know Shah Rukh; my nick name is 'Varsha'. Although I was born in the scorching heat of May, there was a sudden downpour at the time I was born. Every function my parents held for me, whether it was my home coming ceremony—*Barahi Sanskar*, rice feeding ceremony—*Annaprashan* or hair cutting ceremony—*Mundan Sanskar*, it has been graced by the presence of rain in one or the other form. Hence, they named me 'Varsha'.

Call me old school, but I believe rain has always been auspicious for me. It brings me luck and happiness. It could be coincidental, but at every important moment in my life, it had rained either lightly or heavily. I have a positive association with rain. So that evening, when it showered, satisfaction and confidence built in me. I thought it was God's way of telling me: "It is a big day for you tomorrow. Good Luck".

The next morning, I was all pumped up. I was all ready to set the stage on fire, but the only challenge was reaching the destination on time. Travelling from Greater Noida to Ghaziabad does not seem as daunting to me now as it was when I was a student. On top of it, it had poured cats and dogs all night and continued to rain in the morning. I started feeling skeptical about the idea of rain being auspicious to me anymore. My roommate gave up on the idea of attending this recruitment drive because of the extreme weather.

I was determined to attend the event. I reached out to some of my classmates, whom I believed would attend the event. To my astonishment, most of them declined because of the weather. 'How could they be so casual?', I thought.

I contacted the placement coordinator. He informed me about four other students who were eager to attend the interview process but, because of bad weather, could not reach the venue. I collected their names and phone numbers from him and called them personally. Same concern. Bad weather, no conveyance. Despite their concerns, I persisted.

They said if only I could find a taxi to the venue, they could attend the interview. Since all the others, except me, were in the college hostel, they were not allowed to get out in the bad weather for cab search.

It was difficult to find a means of transport to the venue. We usually took a bus from Greater Noida to Ghaziabad bus stand and from there, the sharing autos plied to different colleges. But travelling via bus was out of the question as it was not a direct route and in that rainy weather, there was no guarantee whether we would get the next mode of transport to the venue after getting off the bus.

I am thinking, Shah Rukh, what a relief it is today, that we have Ola, Uber, and other such services. But, that day, I felt like a cat stuck up in a tree. My entire life flashed in front of my eyes. How I had convinced everyone in my family to let me go out and pursue my dreams. Trust me, it is harder than you can imagine. I had tried hard to get admission to an engineering college and had spent many sleepless nights preparing for this day. From the small town of Varanasi to the Jungles of Greater Noida, it was no simple journey for a girl who comes from a conservative family in a small town. My dreams were shattering. I found it hard to breathe.

'How could I let this opportunity slip my hand?' I thought. I could not contain myself anymore. With an umbrella in my hand, I walked down to the nearby taxi stand. It was muddy, and water had logged into different parts of the road. There were only two drivers on the stand, none of them were ready to take a trip to Ghaziabad in that weather. I spoke to them and explained my situation. I tried convincing, pleading, begging, and negotiating, all in vain. Both refused. I was at the mercy of nature.

I looked at my watch. Time was slipping by. Tears welled up in my eyes and as I dragged my step towards my PG in despair, I heard a bleak voice. "*Beta ji, Ruko*".

I turned to see an elderly Sardar ji. He overheard my conversation with the taxi drivers and offered to help us reach the destination. The only condition was he would not do a round trip as he had to proceed somewhere else for some urgent work. I was beyond happy. It felt like I had already won the battle.

I thanked him from the bottom of my heart, boarded the taxi and rushed to my PG to pick up my belongings, documents, and resume for the interview. It took me hardly two minutes to go inside and hop back into the taxi. I tried to make it as quickly as possible.

We then picked up the other four from the college hostel and proceeded towards our destination. While we took a sigh of relief and discussed regarding our preparation, a sense of uncertainty gripped each of us. The uncertainty that despite all these efforts could we make it in time for the interview.

The Sardar Ji would crack jokes occasionally to ease the tension. He then looked at us in the front mirror and said, "*Bachcha Party*! Calm down".

He then fiddled around with his collection of tapes and chose one.

"This one is for motivating you all. This is my favourite," he said, hitting the play button on his car's music system. As he raced the car, the tunes of *Chand Tare Tod Laun* filled the air in the taxi.

The song had its effect. It popped your image into my head and a smile formed on my face.

We reached the venue just in time. We thanked Sardar Ji again for all his help and ran towards the college gates. The process had started, and documents were being collected by the placement coordinators. There were hundreds of students from various colleges and multiple counters were set up to speed up the process. We all queued up to complete the formality.

Once the formalities were done, we were asked to assemble in the auditorium in the next thirty minutes.

We had a breather for half an hour before the actual battle was to begin. I realized I was completely wet. The wet clothes sticking to my body made me uneasy as the realization struck. My ironed pair of clothes were drenched in water and my shiny shoes had trails of mud on the surface and water oozed out of them as I stepped towards the ladies' room. I was worried.

The queue was long outside the ladies' room. Well, it was not a queue per se. The girls gathered as a crowd. Everyone was trying to push the other to get into the changing room. I could hear someone or the other screaming to hurry. Somehow, I managed to get into the crowd but was thrown out by unknown forces. I made two more attempts to get inside but failed.

I looked down at my clothes and shoes; they were a mess. My hand ran through my hair and water poured down. I could not point out what made me more uncomfortable, the hair soaked up in water or the dampness on my feet. 'They would reject me based on my appearance itself,' I thought.

You know Shah Rukh, for the first time in my life I felt so helpless. Opportunity was right in front of me but one after the other things were turning against me. I wanted to scream but as you once said, *'When everything turns against you, just hold on to it for one more moment'*, and so I did.

I decided not to give up without trying, even if it meant appearing in the interview looking like a mermaid.

As I took a few steps towards the auditorium, I heard someone call my name.

"Pree!!" It was a familiar voice.

I turned to find a friend I went to high school with. We studied together from nursery through high school. He was a neighbour and a frequent visitor to my home. He was there to attend the interview, too.

"Hey, what a surprise. How are you?", I said.

"I am good, but you don't seem so, " he pointed at the water dripping down my clothes.

"Yeah, rain!" I smiled, pointing towards the cloudy sky.

"Varsha!", he gave a sarcastic smirk. "Let me help you, " he continued and made a phone call before I could utter a word.

He called his girlfriend who was studying at this college. She took me to her room in the girls' hostel. She offered me a pair of her clothes to change into. I thanked her and changed as fast as I could. I stood in front of the mirror, towel drying my hair, when I found a familiar pair of eyes gazing at me in the mirror. Surprised, I turned back to find you smiling at me. It was one of your posters in her room. Other than your smile, a quote on the poster caught my attention. "*Sometimes winning is everything*".

The quote resonated with me, but before I could dwell on that thought any longer, I got a call from a classmate telling me to hurry. I did the final touch up and rushed back. Time was running out and for a moment I thought, 'What will I do in the interview in this state of mind?'.

'*Sometimes winning is everything*', echoed in my head again. I pulled myself together and walked into the interview room affirming, '*I am the best*'.

There were three rounds, one group discussion, and two interviews. I was dreading the Group discussion. You know, Shah Rukh, being an introvert, I fear this format. Even today.

Anyway, soon it was my turn to face this dreaded format. It was a group of fifteen unknown people, and the interviewer slowly floated the topic for the discussion: the Indian Women's Hockey Team.

As soon as the floor opened for discussion, a lot of comments started pouring in. I was taken aback, kind of in shock, primarily because I am not a sports fan that too, hockey! And again women's hockey!!! Several thoughts started creeping into my mind:

'Should have read the newspaper,'

'Is there a hockey tournament going on?'

'What the hell is this *Chak De*!'

. Anyway, I gathered my thoughts and spoke as much as I could. A few statements I remember were, "Women can do wonders if given equal opportunity and respect"," "Hockey is our national sport and it should be promoted in the same way as cricket" and so on.

Once I got out of the discussion, I heard students humming about *Chak De! India* and Shah Rukh Khan, and how they could make some points because they watched the movie. Shah Rukh, that day, I did not know. Your movie *Chak De! India* has come out and was the basis of this group discussion.

'Shah Rukh! Did I hear Shah Rukh?'

'How come I don't know about this one?', I wondered

Again, before I could give it a thought, I was called for a technical interview. It went on smoothly. I was confident and satisfied with my performance. Next was an HR discussion. I was expecting a pretty lady to be interviewing me for this round, but what I saw in the HR cabin gave me a nervous breakdown.

He was a middle-aged, dark complexion person who hardly fitted into his chair. The tip of his stomach was touching the desk in front of him. While he was scanning through some documents, the *Chandan tilak* on his forehead gave a vibe that he came from the southern parts of India.

When the interview started, he was rude. His questions and tone were harsh enough to make anyone cry. He was loud when he pointed out my documents were dampened. He pulled an annoyed and frustrated demeanor throughout the interview. At times, he would not let me speak, and at other times, he would contradict me ferociously. I thought he was going to eat me for lunch.

I was scared, but I held my composer intact and dealt with the questions as calmly as I could, without breaking into tears. Gradually he softened. He then asked me about how I reached the venue since my college in my resume showed Greater Noida as the location. I briefly narrated how I attended the interview. He then went on inquiring about what motivated me to keep moving, occasionally screaming, "How could you be so careless...", "This is not expected from an engineering student...".

It was a grilling session, and he roasted me like a chicken. I was more worried because it was not an HR interview I had prepared for. He did not ask me any typical HR questions.

The results were to be announced three days later, and I was not sure what to expect.

Honestly, Shah Rukh, as much as I was eager for this job offer, I had already accepted that I had missed this opportunity. I was hopeless and had barely spoken to my parents or friends. And when I spoke, I cursed my fate, the weather, the HR, and God and regretted not taking an interest in sports. "If only I had watched this movie, I would have had a job today," I cursed myself.

The results were announced and to my amazement, I was the only person selected from our group and was one of the two people from my college who got the final offer. It was unbelievable.

I called my dad to break the news to my family. They were so happy. I was the first girl in the family who would work for a multi-national IT firm, Dad called out. He was proud.

"It was a blessing in disguise that you had not watched the movie," Dad said. "The points you made about the Indian Women's Hockey team had a hint of originality. They were not inspired by the movie," he added.

"And the HR, he was not chit chatting with you. He was testing your patience, endurance and persistence," he said. "I am glad you have not taken on to your mother in this regard," he continued, adding a jovial tone to the intense, heartwarming conversation.

"Tell her to go and watch her Shah Rukh's movie," added my mother in the background.

That day, after thanking God and speaking to my mom and dad, I went to watch *Chak De! India*, all by myself. I wanted to spend some time alone with you, thanking you, appreciating you and loving you, for it was you who kept me moving towards my goal inch by inch.

It was the first time I had seen you with beards. Your five o'clock shadow look was breathtaking. You looked exceptional. Throughout the movie, I was forever grateful to you for being with me in every minute of my life.

Today, Shah Rukh, I wanted my sincere gratitude to reach you. On that rainy day, God seemed to test my patience, but the one thing that kept me going was you. Whether it was the soundtrack played by the taxi driver or the quote I needed to read the most, from my quiet affirmations of 'I am the best' to the topic for the group discussion, I felt your presence every second of that day. It was as if you were shielding me from the adversities, providing me courage and strength to face them with a bang. And that is how you, Shah Rukh, became a serendipitous part of my success story. Unknowingly, you have shaped and motivated me in ways I cannot explain.

Love You

Priyanka

I want to Fly

Dear Shah Rukh,

I told you before, my love for poetry began in my teenage years, and you were always at the heart of it. The day I received my job offer, I sat contemplating, reflecting on you, and your journey. I closed my eyes and imagined a twenty-something-year-old Shah Rukh, standing at a crossroads, brimming with dreams and an unshakable fire.

I saw you in a cramped Delhi apartment, poring over scripts, rehearsing lines with the intensity only you could muster. I pictured you pacing on Mumbai's streets, your mind racing with possibilities, your heart pounding with the hunger to make it big. I imagined you standing before a camera for the first time, eyes ablaze with passion, every nerve in your body alive with purpose. I imagined it all.

And as those images filled my mind, I put pen to paper, trying to capture that relentless ambition, that unwavering spirit, your enthusiasm, your zeal. The result was a poem, "I Want to Fly".

It is not just a collection of verses; it is a piece of my heart, a reflection of the dreams I believe once burned within you. In writing it, I felt as if I had stepped into your shoes as if I had traced the path of your aspirations. I am not sure if my words do justice to your story, but I hope, in some way, they resonate with you as deeply as they do with me.

This one is for you, Shah Rukh.

I want to fly

I am all set to
Conquer the sky
With that dream
I want to fly

I want to jump
I want to dive
But most of all
I want to fly

In the endless sky
The clouds go by
And above the clouds
I want to fly

Over the hills
And mountains high
I want to climb

I want to fly

I want to scream
I want to shout
I don't know what
It is all about

With hope in my heart
And dreams in my eyes
I aim too high
I want to fly

Love You,

Priyanka

The Great Recession

Dear Shah Rukh,

Getting a job offer in hand and joining the job are two different things, much like signing a film that never goes into production. The excitement of the offer or signing the deal can be thrilling, but until the project materializes, it is all just potential without execution.

I was excited about having cracked the interview and holding an offer in the third year of my engineering course. The dreams I had woven over the years were about to materialize. I was going to be a free bird, all set to rule the world. The corporate world was calling me and as soon as my last term was completed, I rushed back home to prepare for the new life that was going to unfold.

While I was getting ready to rock and roll, God had other plans for me. The Great Recession hit the world, shattering all my dreams like a glass vase dropped from a towering height.

Do you remember the year 2008, Shah Rukh? Yeah, the year of infinite unfortunate incidents across the globe. The U.S. housing bubble burst sent shock waves to the global economy. Then Lehman Brothers collapsed, causing a financial ripple effect, which brought many of the financial institutions to their knees. Next, the global stock markets crashed. It spiralled out of control.

Millions lost their jobs. Several businesses crumbled. The world seemed to drown in economic chaos. And as if it was not enough, we had the Satyam scandal. One of the biggest corporate scandals that shook the foundation of corporate trust in India. It was like the world collectively held its breath, waiting for the storm to pass.

Yeah, that was the year I graduated. 2008! While I was waiting for an email from my employer confirming the date and location for my joining, I got the news that our joining had been delayed indefinitely. Telephones kept ringing day in and day out, all the batch mates reaching out to each other about the latest updates.

'Did anyone hear from their employers?'

'My employer assigned some online training'

'Are you applying for other jobs?'

'There are no new openings!'

Those were some endless discussions, and the fear of the unknown and uncertainty gripped us. While some of the 2008 pass-outs did not wait and went ahead pursuing a higher degree, girls like me were stuck at home. I tried hard to take up some jobs, full-time, part-time, teaching, and admin but all in vain. There was not much scope in Varanasi and moving out of the city for a job hunt, well, my parents thought it would be too much of a risk than an opportunity. Amidst all this, there started another debate in our family—Marriage!

You know Shah Rukh, in modern India (and yes, I am being sarcastic); we emphasize female education, but once a girl graduates, the first thing her parents think is about getting her married. I do not understand parents' obsession with marrying their daughters early.

"If you don't like me being around you, I will find another home to live in by myself."

"Did you make me an engineer so that you can marry me to a rich NRI and do his laundry and dishes?"

"What about my dreams? I did not study so hard just to be tied to some random idiot."

"I want to do a job and be financially independent. After all, I am no less than the groom you are looking for me."

I have had innumerable tussles with my mother, especially whenever the topic of marriage was discussed. Now, when I think it was their concern for me, an annoying one, though. They wanted to divert my mind with marriage rather than me being depressed by the uncertainty of a career.

To take my mind off those heated conversations, I spent my time playing with my little sister and helping her with homework, brushing up on my basics in case an interview opportunity came up and watching the cartoon network. Then there was a day in my life I could never forget.

It was around 4 pm on a winter afternoon. I was watching the Tom and Jerry show with Ekta, and the aroma that filled the home gave a hint about my mother cooking something delicious in the kitchen. We were so indulged in the show that it did not bother us to find out why she was cooking at this odd hour.

While we were so deeply engrossed in the cartoon that when the doorbell rang, I mindlessly hopped and opened the door, enacting Tom. I made a stupid Tom-like face and mimicked his voice. I was expecting dad. But to my embarrassment, there were two people, one of them I recognized as my father's friend's son and the other one was a new face to me.

I felt so awkward and uncomfortable that I wanted the floor should crack open and I disappeared in that. The two of them smiled as I made way for them, looking down in unease.

I ran back to Ekta and told her what had just happened. We rolled on the floor with laughter and continued our show. Minutes later, my mother called me into the drawing room where the two gentlemen were seated.

"This is Priyanka, our daughter", my mom introduced me to the new face.

"She did her B. Tech from Greater Noida," my dad added.

Shah Rukh, that was the most horrific moment of my life. I looked at my mom and dad in their eyes. The feeling of anger and betrayal radiated from me when I realized Mr. New Face had come to woo me and I was not even aware of it. I felt like a prop, put on display.

I was so infuriated I could not modulate my voice to be calmer and it was apparent from my body language that this situation was not called for. I could not look at Mr. New Face while replying to whatever he was talking about. My gaze was fixed on Mom and Dad, full of resentment.

When the two guests left, my mom asked me for my feedback on Mr. New Face. I was so angry with her that I screamed. She tried to pacify me but two minutes later she too lost her temper, and we had a good squabble. It went to the extent that we did not talk to each other for a week.

When I told Varun about it, who was on a trip to the northeast with friends, he spoke to Mom and Dad. He is the one who is always by my side, no matter what. He understood my dreams and aspirations, my state of mind and what I was going through. When he convinced our parents, they agreed to let me go out and look for a job in Delhi and Noida.

I had a few friends there and was planning to stay there for a week. Yes, a week was what my parents gave me to live the life I wanted.

My father gave me a two-way ticket and told me, lovingly, "Go, see for yourself and, in case you do not get a job, come back home. Otherwise, I will cancel the return ticket."

It was like he was saying, 'Ja Simran ja. Jee le apni zindagi.'

That one week changed my life.

From the day I landed in Delhi, I started taking interviews, mostly at call centres, then there were some computer training institutes where I applied for a trainer's profile, and so on. Surprisingly, I got job offers from every single one of them. In seven days, I had seven offers. Finally, I settled for a call center which paid the most and was in Noida, a place I was much familiar with.

I joined this call center with twenty others and two days later, a new batch of fifteen people joined. Among them was the person who was going to be my friend, my partner and my better half for the rest of my life—The love of my life—Mohit.

Mohit is a person who attracts the opposite gender much like a magnet, even today. Though his charm and wit are something I admire now but my first expression of him was exactly the opposite. I thought of him as one of those backbenchers in the class whose only intention was to annoy others. I believed he was one of those who would chase around girls meaninglessly. Well, I was not entirely wrong.

Our first interactions were also of a rather rocky nature. I did not like him at all, and we ended in disagreements in each of our conversations. He was irritating and a showoff. I took notice of him when, during one of our training sessions, he started speaking about share markets, a subject I just read in high school, and a topic most dreaded during the recession phase. Again, he was being a showoff. Another time he argued with the trainer over a silly topic, and I was very clear that it was his deliberate attempt to boast about himself and humiliate the trainer. I perceived him as an annoying, irresponsible, immature, overly flirtatious and arrogant person during our initial interactions. Some of these perceptions hold true to date.

Mohit would have also found me serious, dull and not his type of girl initially. Though he never opens up about his first impression of me but that is what I can imagine stepping in his shoes. He would annoy me with all his stupid antics.

Anyway, it was not the kind of start that would lead to any sort of connection. But it did. Over time, we saw a more genuine side of each other. We became friends—closer than we had ever expected. Over the next three months, our bond grew stronger, and we shared countless moments that deepened our understanding of one another. But as fate has a way of twisting things, just as our friendship was blooming, I received an email. It was my joining letter from my employer. I was to join my new job in Mumbai in a month.

His look when I broke the news about moving to Mumbai for my joining is still fresh in my memory. His expression that tried hard to hide the disappointment behind a sober smile, but could not, was something I will never forget. It was a mixture of surprises and regret as if he had not expected our time together would be cut so short. He was happy for me, but I could see the weight of the news in his eyes, maybe even a bit of sadness at the thought of me leaving. The moment was brief, but it spoke volumes, and it left me wondering whether he had begun to value our friendship more than I had realized. I wondered how close we had come in just three months.

It was strange, Shah Rukh, the person I hated first, was now so dear to me that the thought of leaving him to pursue my dreams felt like cheating on him. But I did what I had to.

Even after I moved to Mumbai, we never lost touch. We spoke to each other every single day. He was the best friend I ever had. We spoke about our problems and suggested solutions. We discussed our ambitions and goals. He gave me lessons on the share market and even on driving a car. I taught him to cook, all on phone calls! Can you imagine! It would have been during these calls that we started developing feelings for each other, but did not realize it.

You know Shah Rukh, we never had a formal proposal. After a year of work, when my parents again brought up the topic of marriage, I had no reason to say no. When I informed Mohit, he would only get annoyed and say,

"You wanted to go for higher studies, right?"

"What happened to your dreams?"

"How could you marry any random guy?"

When he did not open up about what he wanted, I thought, perhaps, he did not feel the same way for me as I did for him. And I could not marry another person, having feelings for Mohit. I had to suppress all my feelings for him. So, I made up my mind to cut all ties with him. I started avoiding his calls and distancing myself from him entirely. It was difficult, but I had to. When the incoming calls felt daunting and I could not stop myself from giving in to the temptation of speaking to him, I decided to change my number. I bought a new SIM card.

And as if luck might have a different plan, the new sim did not activate for a week! Damn It! Mohit kept ringing. I kept my cell phone mostly silent just to avoid the temptation of picking up his call. One evening, out of the blue, I received a message from Mohit. The words he wrote melted me. He asked me to speak to him one last time.

Little did I know, what I thought was going to be the end of our friendship was going to be the beginning of a lifelong relationship. At that moment, I realized that fate had more in store for us than I could have ever expected.

Shah Rukh, do you remember I told you, DDLJ is my story? Now, do you know why? There are so many parallels between the movie and my life. Like Simran gathered all her courage to ask her father for a month to fulfil her dreams, I had revolted with my parents to get a week to do what I wanted.

Simran met a guy on her trip who she hated initially but finally ended up with, much like I hated when I first met Mohit. The realization that Simran and Raj were in love with each other happened only when they took their separate path, just as we both realized our love for each other when we decided to cut off all connections with each other. The only difference was, there were no Bauji in our story! When we informed our families about our relationship, both our families were supportive of us.

Ever Since I watched you as Raj, Shah Rukh, on my twelfth birthday, I had always wanted a love story like that for myself. I have lived the movie in my mind, scene by scene, over and over, imagining myself to be the Simran, and you as my Raj. But you were already taken, huh! So, God helped me manifest my own Raj in my real life.

Trust me when I say Mohit is the Raj in DDLJ. He is everything Raj stands for, the charm, the humour, the deep sense of love and responsibility. Just like Raj, Mohit has this incredible ability to make you feel special, to make ordinary moments extraordinary. For me, Mohit is not just my partner; he is the living, breathing version of the dream I nurtured after watching DDLJ. In every way that matters, Mohit and Raj are the same.

There are several moments in the movie where I can bet that had it been me and Mohit instead of Raj and Simran, the conversation would have been exactly the same. The emotions, the way the dialogues were delivered, would have been the same if this was a real-life situation with me and Mohit.

On this note, I want to take a moment to express my sincere gratitude to you, Shah Rukh, for you made me understand what I wanted in my life. You made me realize what I truly desired in a partner and inspired me to manifest a love story so eternal in my life, one that feels like it is straight out of a dream—a love that mirrors the passion, intensity, and depth I once admired on screen. For that, I will always be thankful to you.

Love You

Priyanka

Haule Haule

Dear Shah Rukh,

"So, this one goes out to her. This one is for you, mom."

I recently stumbled upon a throwback video on social media. It was a clip of your acceptance speech on receiving your first Filmfare award for Best Debut (Male). In that less than one minute video, I found myself adoring you more than ever. There cannot be a more heartwarming way to express your gratitude and dedication to your mother.

Though it was a happy moment, I could relate to your sorrow of not being able to share a pivotal moment with the one you love the most. I could feel how much you missed your mother and longed for her presence. In that thirty-second speech, I felt your enduring love and your heartfelt tribute to your mother. It must have been a bittersweet moment in your life, Shah Rukh. Though you reached a significant milestone in your life, it was tinged with the void of her absence. That twenty-six-year-old Shah Rukh Khan resonated with me in every way.

I have heard you say this several times, that the greatest agony of your life is your parents could not witness your achievements and success, and you miss them very much. I understand that the happiest moments of your life are when you can bring a smile to your parents' faces. When your parents feel proud of you.

You know, parents are the building blocks of our lives. They lay the foundation for our success. They invest so much of their time, energy, and love into shaping us into the people we become. And when we finally achieve something, the first thought is to share that success with them, to let them know that all their sacrifices, all their efforts, were worth it.

When I received my first salary, all I could think about was my parents. It was not about the money; it was about what it represented, the culmination of their dreams for me, the proof that all their hard work had borne fruit. I wanted to dedicate that first paycheck to them, as a small token of my gratitude for everything they had done for me.

I had recently graduated from college and stepped into the corporate world, full of dreams and aspirations. It was an exciting yet daunting time, as I was eager to make my mark and build a life, I and my parents could be proud of. My first job was with a multinational corporation in Mumbai, a city known for its fast pace, and relentless energy, and a place where millions come to chase their dreams. But as vibrant as the city was, it also posed its own set of challenges.

The starting salary at my job was modest, and as anyone who has lived in Mumbai would know, the cost of living there was overwhelming. From the steep rent for a small apartment to the daily expenses of commuting, food, and other necessities, every rupee mattered. It often felt like the city was a test of endurance, as much as it was an opportunity to grow. Again, you know better. It is your city. You have lived through it. Life was tough in Mumbai.

Mumbai is a city that does not allow you to stand still. The relentless pace of life, the crowded trains, and the hustle and bustle of the streets, it is all a part of the city's character. But for someone new, it can be overwhelming.

Every day for me was a balancing act, trying to keep up with the demands of my job while managing my daily expenses, all the while feeling the weight of being far from home. The city has a way of testing your limits, pushing you to find your own rhythm in its chaos.

I was fresh out of college and was starting a new phase of my life. It was something I had always aspired for. Yet the thrill and excitement of starting a new career were sometimes overshadowed by the nervousness and self-doubt about whether I would fit in or meet the expectations placed on me. In those early days, when the pressure of adjusting to a new life in a demanding city seemed too much to bear, my father's words were a beacon of hope: "You are starting from where I have reached after earning for thirty years."

He said it with such pride and reassurance; it reminded me that the starting point of my journey was something he had worked his entire life to achieve. His belief in me and his reassurance that I was already ahead, that I was standing on the shoulders of all the hard work and sacrifices that he and my mother had made were a powerful reminder that, despite the struggles, I was on the right path, and that every challenge I faced was a stepping stone toward something greater.

Those words gave me strength on the days when I felt like giving up. They made me realize I was not just working for myself, but also carrying forward the hopes and dreams of my family. My dad's pride in my achievements, no matter how small, fueled my determination to keep pushing forward, even when the going got tough.

After six months of working in Mumbai, I took my first vacation. It was a much-needed break, a chance to step back from the daily grind and reconnect with the people who mattered most to me. During those six months, I had been saving diligently from my modest salary, cutting corners wherever I could to put aside a little extra each month. My parents had always been careful with money, teaching me the value of saving and spending wisely. But now that I had some savings of my own, I wanted to do something special for them.

As any child would, I too, wanted to use my first significant earnings to bring a smile to my parents' faces. I wanted to prove to them I had grown up, that I could take care of them in the same way they had always taken care of me. I wanted to give back, even if it was just in a small way, for all the love and support they had showered upon me throughout my life.

Well, they were some far-fetched dreams, Shah Rukh, because the amount of money I could save in those six months was barely enough to take them for an outing. Yet, the zeal to do something for your loved ones, that first step towards financial independence, that first gift from your own money, is a feeling you can feel only once in your life.

So, on a bright Sunday morning, during my vacation, I gathered my courage and announced to my parents, "I am taking you out shopping today, and then we will watch a movie."

I was more than eager to see their response. The unexpected command momentarily stunned them. They were not used to taking orders from me, especially not commands that involved spending money. My mom, in particular, was reluctant. Our family only went to the theatre for special occasions—birthdays, anniversaries, or the release of a highly anticipated film. It was not something we did on a whim.

My mother had always been cautious about spending. Being a typical middle-class mother, she made saving paramount and scrutinized every expense. She instilled in me the importance of saving, wanting me to understand the value of wise spending and avoiding frivolous expenditures. So, when I insisted, we go shopping and watch a movie, she rolled her eyes and tried to brush off the idea.

"Oh please, we are not sitting through your beloved Shah Rukh's nonsense," she said, trying to escape my plan.

My mom has mastered hiding her genuine emotions behind dumb remarks. I could feel the excitement in her voice, but she would not admit it.

"Mom!!" I looked at her in disbelief. "How could you say that?"

She knew how much I adored you but would still test my patience.

But I was determined. This day was important to me, and I wanted it to be perfect. After some convincing, my parents finally agreed to my plan. My heart swelled with excitement, and my eyes twinkled with anticipation. It had been so long since we had spent a day out together as a family, indulging in leisure activities without a care in the world. The thought of spending the day with my parents, and making them happy, brought a sense of joy that I had not felt in a long time.

We spent the entire afternoon shopping. It was a simple yet fulfilling experience. I wanted to make sure we got something for everyone, my father, my mother, and even a little something for my siblings. The joy of picking out clothes, the banter over what looked best, and the shared laughter made the experience even more special. For a few hours, we were lost in our own world, away from the worries of daily life.

After our shopping spree, we headed to the nearby cinema hall to catch a movie. *Rab Ne Bana Di Jodi* was running, and I could not think of a better film to watch with my parents. The movie was heartwarming, and your portrayal of Surinder Sahni was nothing short of adorable.

You looked so darn cute, Shah Rukh. As I watched you on screen, I could not help but compare the simplicity you portrayed on screen to that of my dad. Surinder Sahni's simple attitude and the way he cared for her partner reminded me of the small gestures my Dad would make to please Mom and us. I can bet no one could have done justice with Surinder Sahni other than you.

As the movie played, me and my sister found ourselves enjoying every moment of it, but my mind was focused on my parents. I prayed hard, hoping that they would enjoy the film as much as I enjoyed taking them out for the movie. For the first time, I was more concerned about someone else's reaction to a Shah Rukh Khan movie than my own. I kept sneaking glances at them, trying to gauge their expressions, hoping to see signs of enjoyment. For once, I was more focused on someone other than you during your movie, Shah Rukh.

To my relief, they both seemed to be engrossed in the film. My mother's face, usually so composed, was lit up with a smile, and my father, who rarely showed his emotions, seemed genuinely moved by the story. I could not have asked for a better outcome. But I wanted to hear it from the horses' mouth.

We came out of the theatre smiling. I would sneak a peek at their expressions now and then. I was eager to know their reaction. It was becoming difficult for me to wait any more for their response. However, I pretended to stay calm. My Mom and Dad would exchange glances with each other and smile. My mother's face was eluding a beam of joy, and my Dad still held his calm and composed persona.

After the movie, we headed to a restaurant for dinner. I wanted to make the evening even more special, so we ordered my mother's favourite dishes and my father's favourite desserts.

As we waited for the food to arrive, my father turned to me and said, “You are a grown-up now,” patting me gently on the back.

His words carried a depth of emotion that was hard to put into words. His eyes, usually so steady and composed, were slightly damp, but he maintained his cheerful demeanour. I could feel the weight of pride, love, and a hint of nostalgia in his voice, as though he was seeing not just the person I had become, but also the little girl I used to be. At that moment, the bustling noise of the restaurant seemed to fade away, leaving only the quiet, unspoken bond we shared.

My mother, true to her nature, tried to divert the conversation, perhaps to hide her own emotions.

“Shall I tell you something?” She took a deep breath as her gaze shifted from me to Ekta and then back to me. “The character of Suri in this movie is similar to your Dad.”

It was a sudden shift from an emotional moment to a humorous one. Me and my sister exchanged surprised looks while my mom blushed, and my father felt uneasy in his chair. This was the last thing any of us had expected to hear, and for a moment, the gravity of the moment dissolved into laughter and disbelief.

“Tell us more, Tani partner!” Ekta’s playful laugh echoed as she nudged Mum lightly, her eyes sparkling with mischief.

Dad tapped her head with a teasing grin as if saying, ‘She should know all of this.’

"In our times," mom continued, "The husband and wife expressed their love like this, gently, bit by bit. *Haule Haule!*"

As my sister and I giggled at the revelation, my father joined in, adding his own perspective.

"Yes, it took a lot of effort for me to make your mom take notice of me," he said with a playful smile. His eyes sparkled. I felt it was the memories of the days when he tried to make an impression on Mom.

She could only smile coyly, her usual reserved demeanour giving way to a moment of vulnerability.

As the conversation progressed, they shared a lot of untold stories of their early married life. The scenes on the screen perfectly mirrored the dynamics of the family, with mom diligently preparing lunch boxes for Dad and Dad taking her to fairs and exhibitions. From mom's undivided attention on the household chores to Dad's attempts to capture her interest, every aspect of their daily lives mirrored the scenes you depicted on the screen.

Their words painted a picture of a bygone era, when love found expression in subtle, quiet ways—through small gestures, a shared look, or a simple act of kindness. It was a time when public displays of affection were rare, and people took time to open to their partners. But the love was no less deep or meaningful.

They spoke of the challenges they had faced, the moments of doubt and fear, but also the love and commitment that they had seen them through. Their stories were filled with humour, but also with the wisdom that comes from years of living together, through good times and bad. It was a side of them I had never seen before, and it deepened my appreciation for the bond they shared, and I was all the more grateful to you, Shah Rukh.

I realized that, just like Suri and Tani in the movie, my parents had found their ways of expressing love. They did not need grand gestures or elaborate words, their love was clear in the way they cared for each other; in the small things they did every day. You had given them a chance to reflect on their journey together, and in doing so, had given me a new perspective on the true essence of love.

All the while, although I listened to them intently, in my mind and heart, I could only appreciate you for igniting this conversation. Had you not brought the character of Mr. Suri to life, I would never have heard these untold stories about my parents' experience of love. You had sparked something in them, bringing back memories of their journey together.

While I was lost in your thoughts, admiring you, appreciating you, my spell was broken when in the middle of the conversation, Mom turned to me and said, "The movie felt like, Your Shah Rukh is living our story on screen".

She then looked at Dad, "Did you not feel like her Shah Rukh copied you in this movie?"

"He is a copycat!" she declared, leaning back in her chair comfortably.

Again, this was her attempt to hide her genuine feelings. Her body language made it clear that she was utterly impressed but would not admit it.

It was a fun-filled day. A day of my life imbibed in my heart. How can I ever forget the sparkle in their eyes and the happiness on their faces that evening? The joy that lit up their faces was heavenly. It was a simple yet memorable moment.

I wonder how the love between Surinder Sahni and Tani was as much appreciated by a generation older than us as it was by us.

When public displays of affection were not common, when people took time to open up to their partners, when they made small efforts to impress each other, every time I watch this movie, I cannot help but visualize my parents, grandparents and all my aunts and uncles on the screen. It feels like I am witnessing how love blossomed in their lives. *Haule Haule*!

It is your essence, Shah Rukh. People tend to find parallels between their lives and the character you portray on screen. Their feelings and thought process resonates with Raj, Rahul, Aman and Surinder Sahni. That, I think, is the reason people from all walks of life, from all ages and stages of their lives, consider you as their own.

Shah Rukh, that day was one of the happiest days of my life. It was not just about shopping, movie, or dinner. It was about the time we spent together as a family. It was about the stories we shared, the laughter we enjoyed, and the love that bound us together. The day was a reminder of what mattered in life, and it left me with memories that I would cherish forever.

In the end, my first significant earnings were not about spending money, they were about creating moments that would last a lifetime. The joy of seeing my parents happy, of hearing their stories and sharing in their memories, was worth more than any material possession. And as I lay in bed that night, reflecting on the day, I could not help but feel grateful for the family I had, and for the love that we shared.

Shah Rukh, that outing was important to me for two reasons. First, I realized that happiness is about acknowledging the role our parents play in our lives, about making them a part of our victories, no matter how big or small. And just like you dedicated your first award to your mother, I too silently dedicated my first savings to my parents. It was my way of saying, "This one is for you, Mom and Dad. Thank you for everything."

Second, I was excited—little by little, your magic had started working on mom too. *Haule Haule*!

Love you

Priyanka

Manattein

Dear Shah Rukh

When I was asked in my job interview about the preferred job location, the only place that popped up in my head was your city. Mumbai.

Mumbai—The city that never sleeps, where dreams are an integral part of daily life, has always been a land of endless possibilities. For millions, it is a place where aspirations come alive, where the pursuit of dreams is an unyielding force.

People call it a city of dreams. People come to Mumbai with a lot of dreams and make them happen too. Who would be a better example than you, Shah Rukh? You came to Mumbai with nothing but a dream to rule the city, and today, you reign not only over the city but also over the hearts of millions around the world. King Khan!

For me, Mumbai was more than just a city; it was the place where I hoped to realize two of my deepest desires. Do you remember the boy from school I mentioned earlier? My first crush. I got to know he was in Mumbai, and for some strange reason, I thought I should find him. Little did I know, in a city like Mumbai, it was nearly impossible to find someone without a hint of where to look for. Yeah, I am often driven by emotions; I cannot let go of anyone easily.

But the bigger reason was, it was your city. It was where “Mannat” materialized, and stood tall, symbolizing your journey from a dreamer to a king. I was hopeful my *mannat*, too, would come true someday. It was a city that brought me closer to you. Being in your city and having the opportunity to catch a glimpse of the man who rules my heart always sent my adrenalin levels soaring high, as if existing near you was an incomparable sensation. It felt like I was part of something extraordinary, something larger than life.

From 2009 to 2011, Mumbai was my home. Then, I got married and moved to Chennai. More on that later. The days in Mumbai were the golden period of my life, filled with unforgettable memories and adventures.

We were a group of six friends from different corners of India, brought together by the magnetic pull of Mumbai and the demands of the job. Each of us had our own reason for choosing this city. Some craved independence, wanting to step out of their protective cocoon and experience life on their terms. Others longed to stay close to home, finding comfort in being near family. For some, Mumbai was the ultimate playground, a city buzzing with energy and excitement. For others, it was a land of endless possibilities where dreams could take flight.

Everyone had their reason. Mine? Well, you already know.

While on the one hand, our days went by taking the college to corporate sessions, our evenings were a pure struggle for finding a roof over our head, after the fifteen-day free accommodation period was over. We spent nights talking to each other and building a lifetime bond, and our weekends were a whirlwind of excitement, dancing at clubs, catching the latest movies, and exploring every nook and corner of the city.

Playing *Aankh Micholi* in bustling shopping malls, pranking random passers-by during *Truth Or Dare* games, and singing *Antakshari* by the serene Powai Lake were a few activities we indulged in. We would act out in Dumb Charades at the iconic Nariman Point. From Hiranandani to Juhu Beach, Lokhandwala to Bandstand, Mumbai was our playground, and I do not remember a place where we were not chased away by the police at 3 a.m., their batons swinging in the air as we laughed and ran. But amid all the fun, one thing remained constant—my unfulfilled dream of meeting you, Shah Rukh.

In those two years, I attended countless events, visited several clubs, and saw a lot of celebrities. I met some singers, a few actors, and even some sports people. But the one person for whom I was in Mumbai, the one I longed to see, did not appear anywhere. Where were you, Shah Rukh, during those two years?

Call me insane, but every time I stepped out, I was hopeful of seeing you somewhere, as if the world might part, and you would walk right into my life. And then, my heart would break when you did not. My friends, aware of my obsession, started teasing me relentlessly. They would point at random people and scream, “Priyanka, look, it’s your Shah Rukh!” My heart would skip a beat, only to sink with disappointment moments later.

However, my spirits remained high. I thought, if I want to meet you, I should visit Mannat. What if luck shines on me and fulfils my wish? Silly me! With that hope in my heart, I convinced my friends to accompany me to Mannat. Well, not just convinced, I bribed them!

When I first asked my friends to accompany me to Mannat, they laughed out loud. They would tease me endlessly, but I knew it came from a place of love. They understood you were more than just a celebrity to me. You were an inspiration, a symbol of what one could achieve with passion and determination. Despite this understanding, friends are friends! They only agreed to visit Mannat when I offered them that the next Shah Rukh Khan movie would be my treat to them.

It was my twenty-fifth birthday and with the dream of meeting you, the six of us came to Mannat. I became ecstatic as soon as we got there. I had a hard time controlling myself as I gazed at the grand gates of your majestic bungalow, imagining you were just beyond them.

We approached the guards, pleading with them to tell us if you were home and if we could catch even a fleeting glimpse of you. Wanting to know about your schedule, we inquired about when you usually come or go for the shooting, so that we can see you, even from afar.

I tried every trick in the book, claiming it was my birthday, inventing a chronic illness, and even suggesting I might not live to see my next birthday. It was all dramatic, but I am a terrible actor. You know Shah Rukh, your guards are so well-trained, I must say. They laughed and giggled, but they did not budge, and eventually, they shooed us away.

But I was not about to let my birthday end in disappointment. So, right there, in front of Mannat, we celebrated. My friends brought out a birthday cake, and as I closed my eyes to make a wish, I felt a strange connection to you, Shah Rukh. I felt your presence in the air. I believed you were just a few feet away, on the other side of the walls, looking over me. On my special day, I believed you were with me. Tears welled up in my eyes, not out of sadness, but out of sheer joy and gratitude for this moment, even if it was only in my imagination. My friends hugged me tightly. It was an emotional moment for me, and their support meant a lot.

Your guards were not even interested in sharing our cake, *Khadoos*! Finally, we decided to spend the rest of the night at Juhu Beach.

"Hey guys, let's not go home tonight and watch the sunrise over the ocean," I suggested, filled with the kind of optimism that only comes from a night spent near your hero's home.

The five others gave back a surprised look.

"What? It will be fun," I insisted.

"Don't you want to go home today?" asked one of them. "You have a production release tomorrow, right?"

"I think she wants to keep an eye on Mannat, in case she can spot her Shah Rukh." poked another as if reading my mind.

"Why don't you try for a job vacancy at Mannat, for the position of a guard," teased the third one.

"Her sun and the moon and the entire universe is behind the walls of Mannat," and the banter went on. We laughed our lungs out, as they did not leave any opportunity to embarrass me.

Our conversations revolved around you, sometimes serious, sometimes silly. My friends would joke that if they ever lost me in a crowd, all they had to do was to scream your name unanimously, and there I would be. They were not entirely wrong.

We played games and laughed, waiting eagerly for the first light of dawn at Juhu Beach. We sat on the sand looking into the endless water, waiting for the sunrise. Every time the waves hit the shore; I could not help but wonder what it would be like watching a sunrise with you.

It was getting brighter, and we were eagerly waiting for the sun to rise from behind the waters in the ocean.

A few minutes later, one of my friends turned back, and sighed, "And Here comes your Sun".

For a moment I felt it was a variation of teasing session where they point to random strangers screaming—here comes your Shah Rukh! We all turned, and the sun was blinking from behind the high-rise buildings to the other side of the beach. We instantly realized that Juhu Beach is on the west coast, and we cannot witness a sunrise here. Only sunsets!

That was one memorable night. The fact I was hardly a few feet away from you, though outside the wall of your home, made it special for me. I wish I had a camera back then to capture the moment. However, this moment remains forever captured in my heart.

Despite all my efforts, I never got to meet you, Shah Rukh, during my time in Mumbai. My friends teased me endlessly about my obsession, but they also understood that it was more than just a celebrity crush. You were a stimulus for my aspirations; a symbol of what dreams could achieve. My love for you was not just about the movies or the roles you played; it was about the values you represented, and the hope you give to so many.

You know, Shah Rukh, I came to Mumbai to meet two people and met none of them. Even though I did not find my school-time crush or met you, Mumbai gave me something else. It gave me friendship, adventure, and memories that will last a lifetime. And the belief that if you want something with all your heart, the universe will conspire to make it happen.

And I can say so because a few years later, I got hold of my schoolmate on a social media platform; we are friends now and speak to each other more often than not. I have not met him yet as he is in another part of the country, but I believe our paths will cross someday.

Now, it is your turn. I have a firm belief, "*agar kisi cheez ko dil se chaho, to puri Kaynaat use apse milane ki koshish mein lag jaati hai*".

Someday, I believe this is going to happen. I am going to meet you and not just as a random fan. The forces in the universe have fulfilled everything I truly desired and I am sure, one day I will get to witness a sunrise with you, Shah Rukh, and share a tale or two about the crazy girl who celebrated her birthday outside Mannat. Until then...

Love You

Priyanka

The Shah Rukh Charm

Dear Shah Rukh,

> *"Kaun kehta hai ki chamatkar nai hote. Mujhe dekho, kareeb se dekho, aur tumhe chamatkar dikhai dega."*

Let us talk about magic today. You know, you have a magical charm that people get attracted to you like a magnet. No one can harbour dislike or hard feelings towards you for long. Eventually, anyone who has a little goodness in their heart gets drawn to you like a moth to a flame. You have that charisma that can move any heart. How do you do that, Shah Rukh?

I am dying to know what your secret is. I wish I knew how to make my colleagues like me instead of competing with me and I wish my managers understood I was always on their team and not trying to sabotage their meetings. Forget that, sometimes I think even my mother does not like me. She keeps annoying me and gets annoyed with me for anything and everything. Can you take some crash course for me on 'How to Win Every Heart', please? Ahh, sure you can. Can You? Please?

While you make up your mind about this proposal, let me tell you about an incident. It was no less than some magic.

Those days I was in Mumbai. It was my first job, and I was trying to do my best. The only area of my focus was work, as the project had a strict deadline. I was busy as a bee. I was so occupied that I often lost track of time, not realizing when morning turned into evening. The weather felt the same both inside and outside the office. Mornings flew by, transitioning seamlessly into nights. It had been such a long time since I had witnessed an evening.

My stress and frustrations had peaked at their highest level. On the one hand, there were strict deadlines and on the other hand, the web application we developed would not work as expected. Sometimes deployments failed and other times the servers would crash. Where I worked relentlessly to achieve the project deliverables, my manager gave me left and right in the quarterly review meeting. For those three months, there had been nothing exciting in my life until I got a call from my mom one evening.

It was a usual check-in call she would make, but the conversation we had was quite unusual. She started asking me about how life was, how was work and so on. Then she went on lecturing me on taking care of my health, and the importance of work-life balance. To me, whatever she spoke sounded like blah, blah, blah and blah! Every word she uttered was getting on my nerves.

Okay, I must admit; she was concerned about me, and I was being badass. But I was young blood, overworked with responsibilities, trying hard to fit into the new lifestyle with work, work and more work. At one point in our conversation, I got very annoyed and asked her to stop nagging me.

But mothers are mothers, they will not stop. They have a sixth sense for their children. They mysteriously know what is going on in the child's mind and how to increase their dopamine levels. I know this now, as a mother myself, but back then, it was unbearably irritating. Sensing I was not in a good mood and low on energy, she changed the topic.

"Okay, let it be. Tell me this, there is a new movie, your Shah Rukh is starring in. Did you watch it or not?"

"No Mom, " I could barely modulate my voice to hide my frustration, " I don't even get time to sleep or eat, and you are asking me about the movie." I was furious, looking at the project backlog on my computer screen.

She took a deep breath. "Go and watch. It is a good one."

"What is the matter with you?" I snapped at her, "You don't even like Shah Rukh. Why the hell are you bothered if I watched his movie or not?".

I kind of got angry, "I am on the verge of a do-or-die situation, have not slept for days, am overworked and you are rubbing salt on my wounds." I felt like banging my head on the wall and throwing away the laptop and the cell phone.

"Well, I never thought I would say this," she said, taking a deep breath.

"It is indeed a good movie. And your Shah Rukh did a fantastic job portraying the character of Rizwan Khan," her words took me by surprise.

For the next few minutes, she praised you briefly, but all I heard in my head was *'Shah Rukh is the best'*.

"Since when do you care about Shah Rukh?" I softened. It was a sweet surprise for me and for a while, my preoccupied mind drifted to something that kind of had a soothing effect.

"Hmm, He is good," she said, trying hard not to make it a big deal.

"I was moved by his performance in *My Name is Khan*. No one else could have carried that role better." She admired you.

"So, you liked him?", I was inquisitive, as if she had approved of my boyfriend.

For the first few minutes, she refrained from expressing her admiration for you, but then she could not hold back. She went on and on speaking a great deal about you and the way you enacted in *My Name is Khan*. She painted a vivid picture describing how you could depict the innocence of Rizwan Khan and how she was in tears with every scene she saw.

"You always say he has some kind of magic in his eyes. Well, I have started noticing it now," she continued, "I loved the way he..."

"Okay. Enough. Stop it now," I trailed her off, "I want no more spoilers. I will watch this movie once my project goes to production next week."

My heart felt warm, and the tension seemed to dissipate into the air.

"You were right," she continued, "If anyone can give Amit Ji a tough competition, it is your Shah Rukh. No one else has that talent."

It was then I realized that everyone, including family, relatives, cousins, and friends, always refer to you as "*Tumhara Shah Rukh*", "*Your Shah Rukh*". Oh, I am blushing as I pen these words.

Anyway, back to the conversation with Mom. She went on praising and admiring you endlessly. I looked at the watch and it was one and a half hours of my mom praising you. A crescent formed in my face. I was amazed and amused, both at the same time. I had not seen my otherwise finicky mom so much in awe of someone. A feeling of satisfaction sank in. I was happy. My mother had started liking the person I admired the most. It meant a lot to me.

For that one and a half hours, my heart was filled with all sorts of positive feelings. The tension, worry, and annoyance all seemed to have melted away. I felt warm within as if you had embraced me into a loving hug comforting me. The conversation wrapped around my thoughts like a cozy blanket, providing much-needed solace and reassurance, gently lulling me into a peaceful slumber. I slept instantly.

When I woke up, the memory of the conversation with Mom was still fresh and I was energetic more than ever to face my challenges at work.

That day, talking about you was all that I needed. The mere mention of your name is enough to wash away all my stress, frustrations, and tiredness. You increase my oxytocin levels. Shah Rukh, you are my energy boosters. You are my happy hormones. Speaking about you, discussing you and dreaming about you can melt all the tension in the surrounding air. You are the ray of hope in all my sorrows; you are my strength in my lows, and you are the one who can bring a smile to my face in the darkest hour. What do you say, Shah Rukh—"*Bas Naam hi Kafi Hai*".

And now you had a fourth admirer in our family. Isn't it magical? My mother, who, honestly, is very hard to please, now adores you more than me, I think. Ever since the day she watched *My Name Is Khan*, she turned from a critique to an ardent fan. And then there is an eager learner too, Shah Rukh. Could you please teach me some of your "The Shah Rukh Charm"? What Say?

Love You

Priyanka

A Promise Forever

Dear Shah Rukh,

Tell me one thing, what is your take on marriage? People think marriages are beautiful events. Especially in India, it is so colourful, so vibrant and so loud that sometimes people miss seeing the insecurities of the bride. They cannot hear what the girl might want to say.

As a child and even till my adulthood, I always thought marriages were scary. It was like uprooting a delicate plant, which had just started to blossom and plant it in a foreign environment and then expect it to bear fruit immediately. Even when we get a new puppy in our home, we nurture it, take care of it and wait until it has started trusting us and starts growing. But the expectation from a bride is to grow into a woman from a girl overnight.

I always thought about how one could leave one's family and make someone else's family their own. Why should my family be the second priority? The people who made me into what I am today should always come first, right? And why is there so much disparity in marriage?

Times might have changed now, but twenty years ago, those thoughts haunted me whenever we discussed marriages. I think marriage was the scariest and the most challenging thing I ever did in my life. I was so shaken that two days before my marriage, I called Mohit and asked, "Do you really want to get married, or should we call it off?"

It was 24th November 2012. I was getting married. Though the Simran in me had found her Raj, I was still shaking in my boots. The thought of committing to a person with all my heart and soul was daunting. Though me and Mohit dated for three years before marriage, it was mostly a long-distance relationship, with him being in one part of the country and me being in Mumbai. Having a long-distance relationship and living under the same roof were different things, and I was turning cold feet.

The commitment issue was one thing. I also had separation anxiety. Anxiety that I could not see my parents as often. Anxiety that I will be torn between my siblings and my husband. What if I am not heard or understood? What if Mohit does not understand my feelings about you? I did not want to lose my individuality to be known as Mrs. Mohit Vahal.

A day from my childhood flashed through my mind. What if Mohit is a Jonty Rhodes fan and not a Shah Rukh Khan fan? The childhood fear of not being able to express myself, the fear of rejection and invalidation and the fear of not being accepted as I am, was surfacing again.

To top that, as in every Indian wedding, the last-minute *Siyyappa* had to happen. As if it was inevitable. There were angry Fufa Jis and overdramatic in-laws' family. On one hand, there were untidy rooms in the banquet hall and on the other hand, someone was careless enough to drop a lit incense stick, the kind we use in *poojas*, on the mattress almost causing a fire. The Mehandi artist even stole my cell phone. Could you believe that, Shah Rukh?

"Why the hell am I getting married?" the thought constantly kept nagging me. However, my support system, Mom, Dad, Varun and Ekta stood by my side, making sure I do not have a panic attack.

With every step I took towards the marriage hall, the cries from the past echoed louder.

"Why does being older and a girl matter?"

"You always tell me to be the bigger person."

"I feel like I am always the one giving up what I love."

"Why does everything I love have to come second to everyone else?"

"Do I even matter in this house? Am I invisible? Do I have any value for anyone, Dad?"

I froze momentarily before stepping onto the stage. The ice was broken when Mohit cradled my hand and pulled me up.

As the night progressed, all the rituals were performed. Mohit made all efforts to make me, and my loved ones, feel comfortable. He kept cracking jokes to make the intense environment lively. But my own insecurities and fears of the unknown choked me up. I wanted to run away.

When our *saat phere* and *saat vachans* were done, I felt trapped.

Out of anxiety and nervousness, I whispered in his ears, "I need one more promise from you," sweat drops appeared on my forehead on that chilling winter night.

"What happened?" he touched my forehead to check for fever.

"Promise me, you will be a Shah Rukh fan forever and not a Jonty Rhodes fan." I did not know what else to say. There was so much going on inside me, but only these words tumbled out.

"What?", he was certainly not expecting this.

"You will not stop me from loving Shah Rukh more than you," I said, my index finger pointing to him, though shaking.

"And..." I was struggling for words to convey my emotional breakdown but failed miserably.

"And you will not be jealous of him, too. You ought to love him," I continued while losing control over my hands, which just fumbled in the air.

'What am I saying!' I thought in my head.

While Mohit could only give me a shocked look, I started again to command the situation, "And... And... You will take me to watch all Shah Rukh Khan movies in the first week of release, if not the first-day first show," my voice trembled, and I felt a knot in my stomach.

He squeezed my hands, "Are you all right?".

I was shivering. "I don't know," I really did not know.

"All I want is for you to accept the fact that I love Shah Rukh more than you and he will always be my love forever." I could not hold back my tears anymore.

He put his hands on both my shoulders and shook me gently as if trying to wake me up from a horrible dream.

"What is wrong with you?" he was concerned. "Did anybody say something to you?" he asked, wiping the teardrops from my face.

I removed his hand slowly, "No, no," I said hastily, "Promise me, you will not change the TV channel if I am watching Shah Rukh."

Mohit looked at me, smiled and said, "Sure. I Promise".

I opened my mouth to say something more, but as my gaze locked on his, I could not hold it anymore. I cried rivers of tears. He gave me a side hug, allowing me a moment of vulnerability while I wept, not able to understand the emotions churning in me.

Now, when I think back on the day and my behaviour, I find it silly. But was it? It wasn't. I was entering a new phase of life, full of nervousness. In a society where marriage often demands compromises, I fear I might lose my individuality. My identity and interests were at stake in a commitment like this. Assurance and unconditional acceptance were what I was looking for. I was seeking to be accepted with all my quirks and to be allowed to express what I felt.

It was an emotional rollercoaster of stepping into a lifelong commitment. And in all this, you, Shah Rukh, served as a lifeline amid my emotional upheaval, grounding me in something familiar and safe. You were my way of getting my voice heard and understood. And as Varun puts it, 'The Shah Rukh Khan Effect' was in action on my wedding night.

Getting married was the scariest thing I did. Of course! It was an irrevocable change in my life. But with Mohit by my side, it felt a little less daunting. He has always been supportive and did not rush me into anything, giving me time and space to grow into a partner and a friend.

The sense of support became even more important as we started our new life together. One week after the wedding, we moved to Chennai. Mohit was working for a National Bank and was posted in Pondicherry, and I took a transfer from my employer to Chennai. My welcome to this tiny apartment was the same as you welcomed Rani Mukherjee in *Chalte Chalte*, except that his flat was much cleaner than yours in the movie.

He stood me up at the gate, went inside, and when he opened the gate, I found a glass of rice and an oil lamp, the kind we use for *Aartis*, in his hand and talcum powder all over the floor. What could have been a sweeter gesture than this? I was sure I had married a Shah Rukh in real life. I felt safe. He was (and is) my happy place.

However, even after marriage, it felt like we had a long-distance relationship. We had been married for fifteen days, and I was living alone in a place where I knew no one. No one knew me. Neither did I know the language nor the city. The people and the culture, everything was new. It was different. I did not step out of my apartment except for going to the office or getting groceries. Oh! I missed my Mumbai life. This was the exact opposite of what I had in Mumbai. My husband, because of whom I left Mumbai and came to Chennai, lived 200 km away and visited me only once in a fortnight. What rubbish!

Those were gloomy days and my only keep-up was you, Shah Rukh. A small collection of your movies, songs, and interviews was all that I had in Chennai. I would play them continuously from Friday night till Monday morning, repeatedly for several weeks. I would spend time reading about you online, your life journey, controversies and struggles. In short, my free time, my me-time all revolved around you. Over a long weekend, I remember watching one of your movies repeatedly for three days. Insane, right?

On one of the Friday nights, when I returned from the office, I found the door open. I was scared. Gathering all my courage, I entered my apartment and was searching for the switchboard when the lights were dramatically switched on with confetti, flowers and music. Mohit came a day earlier than planned and arranged this romantic date night. After we had dinner, he said, "I have another surprise for you". I was keen. He turned on the laptop and played a downloaded version of *Jab Tak Hai Jaan*.

Shah Rukh, I will admit, I was disheartened and completely annoyed. The warmth I felt because of his showing up a day early seemed to have diminished. I wanted to go out and watch this in a theatre. One, because I felt imprisoned within the four walls of the house, and second, because it was you. However, given all the effort he had put into this evening, I tried to keep calm and continued.

As the movie continued, as always, I could not control my heart, which was beating for you louder than ever. I am sure, sitting next to me, Mohit could hear my heart throbbing in my chest. An hour into the movie, and I could not control myself.

I looked at Mohit. "You know what," I said, "We will watch this at the cinema tomorrow."

I pulled down the laptop screen, which was still playing the movie.

"You know, we have very little time. I will be travelling back tomorrow." He looked at me to express his concern.

"We have an audit on Monday, and we already watched more than half the movie," he tried convincing me.

"But honey, you promised. Please," I pleaded.

It took little for me to get him to give in. You know how it is with newlyweds, there is something irresistible about that charm in the early days when every little gesture feels like an invitation.

Rubbing his forehead, he looked at me and said, "Okay, sweetie. Your wish is my command, Jab Tak Hai Jaan."

The next day, he rescheduled his journey for early morning Monday, and we watched *Jab Tak Hai Jaan* in the theatre. I felt heard and understood. I was happy.

You know, Shah Rukh, there are moments in life when we feel vulnerable, when we want to say something, but the words just do not come out; when we want to take action, but something inside holds us back. It is those 'To be or not to be' state of mind. In those difficult times, we are desperate for the smallest source of support that helps us navigate the emotional turmoil and overcome the challenges life has thrown in our faces.

You know what they say: *Doobte ko tinke ka sahara kafi hota hai.* In every sinking moment of my life, you have been that 'tinka'—my source of hope and strength. I find my voice in you. I rely on you to assert myself. You are the heartbeat of my existence..

Love You.

Priyanka

To You, I Owe It All

Dear Shah Rukh,

Life is full of twists and turns. We never truly know what the next moment holds, yet we dream, we plan, and we build hopes for a brighter tomorrow. We imagine the perfect vacation, the ideal home, and countless other possibilities, unaware of what fate has in store. Like everyone else, I had my plans—plans I believed in, plans I held close—until life unfolded in ways I never expected.

As I moved up the ladder in my career and progressed in my personal life, my dreams grew bigger, too. I wanted to own a magnificent house, a black BMW, a cute little pet, and two kids who would run around the house and colour it with their beautiful memories. I visualized myself as a corporate leader, a loving wife, a dutiful daughter, and the most adorable Mum. Wanting to be rich, famous and beautiful was one thing, but I also wanted to be humble, respectable and modest. I wanted everything in life.

And then, life happened. There came a point in my life when I thought, is it worth it? I started to question my existence. Nothing seemed to make sense. I succumbed to despair, hopelessness, and self-pity. I was like a ship sinking in a stormy sea with no signs of rescue.

All this started when we thought of expanding our family. It had been five years since we got married. It was the time we had planned to have babies. But as easy as it sounded, we were not as fateful. Life had something else in store for us. Something much more complicated than we ever thought.

The journey towards motherhood was challenging. And constant social pressure, sarcastic comments, taunts and *free ka gyan*, made an already stressful journey a more difficult one. And then hit the Covid.

Do you remember the first lockdown, Shah Rukh? Everything came to a halt during the first three months. How did you spend your time during the first lockdown period? With banging the plates to lightening up the oil lamps, it seemed like a celebration to some, while others struggled to commute back to their homes with no means of transportation available. People learned new skills. Some men entered the kitchen for the first time while some women could not come out of the kitchen for the entire day, fulfilling the demands of all the family members now dancing on their heads. People stuck in hostels learned survival instincts. Some did not take it seriously, and some were over-concerned about the lockdown. It was an uncommon experience for everyone.

I wondered how people were getting time to prepare *Jalebis* at home. I barely had time to eat while managing household chores, office commitments, feeding stray animals and running to my gynaecologist. The "work from home", "work from anywhere", and "flexible work hours" were a complete disaster for me. I am telling you; it was the complete opposite of what it was expected to be.

People at home would say, "At least you don't have to go to the office."

And people at the office would say, "Well, at least you don't have to come to the office."

While family members assumed that staying home meant life was easier, as there was no need to commute to the office, the managers at the office assumed that working from home was a luxury.

It was a situation where neither side fully understood the actual challenges of balancing work and home life without one interfering with the other. And no matter where I worked from, people around me downplayed the effort I was putting in. I mean, did everyone think working from home gives me extra hours in a day?

Nonetheless, the time between 2020 and 2022 was very unsettling. With Covid and lockdown, life had come to a standstill. While everyone was trying to make peace with the first wave, the second wave came in, even stronger. There were hues and cries everywhere. All the negativity in the news and the pace at which we were losing our loved ones were heart-ripping. It was a time when incoming calls felt scary. It was a time when 'no news' was indeed 'good news'.

It was also a time I had conceived after years of trying and multiple failed fertility treatments. A time when years of heartbreak, resilience and unanswered prayers finally seemed to pay off. This was the moment I was supposed to be happy, to celebrate and to relax. But all I could think of was what I could do to help my family and friends.

Humanity has never been as helpless as it was during those times. There were no beds available in the hospitals. There was a shortage of oxygen cylinders. People were dying everywhere. Everyone across the globe was impacted by the pandemic and so was I. I was detected as Covid positive. My parents and Ekta, who had just recovered from the same deadly disease, were staying with me.

You know Shah Rukh, in my family, everyone looks up to me as the pillar of strength. They consider me as the one who holds it all together, no matter what. I rarely panic and am the most stable of them all. So, when I contracted the virus, I quietly isolated myself from the family without making a big deal out of it. I did not realize when this physical isolation turned into emotional distancing, too.

All the time, I would pull a jolly face, but something inside me was dying. I was worried about my pregnancy. The baby growing in my belly, day by day, was a part of me, yet felt so fragile, so vulnerable. I tried to stay strong, but the fear of the unknown gnawed at me. What if something went wrong? My body wasn't strong enough. What if I failed to protect this little life before it even saw the world?

I did not let anyone see my fears. I laughed, I joked, and I assured everyone that I was fine. But deep inside, I was crumbling. Three days after my home isolation, what I dreaded the most happened. I miscarried my baby. My oxygen levels dropped drastically. I needed medical care, but we did not have the resources.

Mohit and Ekta made several calls and finally arranged a bed for me in a Covid hospital in Ghaziabad. While arrangements were made to get me admitted to the hospital, my father, who had just recovered from this infectious virus, had a heart stroke—an aftereffect of Covid. There was panic in my house. The ability to think and act at that moment seemed to have diminished. Everyone was paralyzed with fear. But Mohit kept his calm. He had to. He had no other option.

There were two patients in the home and just one person to attend to them both. It was impossible to carry me and my father in the same vehicle. Mohit arranged an ambulance for me. With my father and sister in his car, he drove to the Covid hospital in Ghaziabad first and got me admitted. He then rushed to another hospital in Delhi to get my father treated.

They reached the hospital in time and his treatment started. In the next 2 days, the doctors conducted angiography and angioplasty on my father.

By God's grace, my father recovered and, with all the efforts the doctors and nurses put in the Covid ward, I started responding to the treatment. I bow down to the courage and dutifulness of the medical people. With the right treatment, I could overcome the physical pain, but the emotional suffering of losing a part of me was tearing me apart.

Losing my baby and my father's stroke had struck me in a place so deep within it felt like my very soul had been shattered. I was broken to the core. A feeling of helplessness and guilt washed over me. I blamed myself for not being cautious and getting infected. I blamed myself for miscarrying my baby. The pain was excruciating, both physically and mentally. Neither could I bear the emotional trauma, nor could I share this pain with anyone. I had lost all interest in life. Though alive, I felt dead. Every minute I was awake, I had self-destructive thoughts. Life had lost its meaning.

While in hospital, I got several calls from family, friends and colleagues, but I hardly took any. When Mom called, I only spoke about my father's well-being. I did not feel like speaking about myself. Ekta would try to make jokes in her naughty childlike style to hear me smile, all in vain.

Varun would send me pictures of our childhood days saying, "You remember these events? Or has Corona affected your memory too?"

Mohit had his usual way of showing his emotion. He would often say, "Please hurry back! Your parents are a full-time job, and I am not getting paid for this."

Everyone tried to cheer me up, but I was dead inside.

I was stuck in the Covid ward for 3 weeks. There was no escape. There was not even a window open in the room. We never knew if it was morning or night, sunny or rainy. There were three patients in every room. We could not step out of the room. Now and then I heard someone screaming. Nurses were screaming at the patients for not listening to them. Patients were screaming in pain, or when they saw their fellow patients in pain. Negativity filled the air and my heart and mind too.

One night in the hospital, I could not sleep. Some disturbing and suicidal thoughts kept creeping into my mind. The image I had painted in my mind of a supermom, of the most adorable mother-baby duo, would pop up to shatter in a few minutes. The sarcasm I had faced over the years and the thought that I was going to be barren forever kept me tossing and turning in my bed. "How could you do this to Mohit?" a voice kept haunting me. I wanted to finish the pain once and for all.

While I was on the verge of taking a drastic step, another patient in my room turned on the TV. It was mute as the third one was sleeping. She scrolled for a few minutes and stopped on a news channel. I could not bear the news for one entire minute and requested her to change to something else. She casually tossed the remote and turned her back towards me and slept.

I kept scrolling the channels mindlessly for some time and then stopped at one of them. It was playing *Kal Ho Na Ho*. I had watched this movie several times earlier. But that day, it changed me and my perspective on life. I watched the entire movie on mute. That day, I did not watch the movie, I watched a dying man. A man who knew he could not make it but still was not ready to give up on life. A man who himself did not have enough time to live yet wanted to make the most of it. I watched a man who knew he would not be a part of it yet left no stone unturned for his loved ones to be happy.

You know Shah Rukh; *Thoughts are something you cannot control. They drift towards whom they like when they like.*

As I watched Aman Mathur fight against all odds with a smile, my mind drifted to you, Shah Rukh, not just as the actor playing him but as the man who has battled his own share of struggles. In my mind's eye, I saw a fifteen-year-old boy grappling with the unbearable loss of his father, forced to grow up too soon. I pictured a young man of twenty-five, his hands folded in desperate prayer, clinging to hope as his mother wavered between life and death. I visualized a little brother, carrying the weight of responsibilities far beyond his years, shielding his sister from the harsh realities of life while silently battling his own fears

I was reminded of the wounds life has inflicted upon you, some visible, others buried deep within, and yet, you embraced them all with grace. I sobbed some silent tears for I could feel the pain you went through.

And then, as I closed my eyes, I felt your embrace around me, as if you were whispering in my ears: *Pree, life is transient. You are not immortal. One day you have to go, but till then you can try to live in the present. God has been kind to you by surrounding you with people who genuinely care for you. It is on you how you cherish these people and their love. You cannot give up on life. Life will always be full of challenges and the only way to overcome those is by being resilient and positive.*

Those thoughts provided me with peace and gave me strength. I started noticing people around me in the hospital. The nurses who came to take blood samples early in the morning, the doctors who kept fighting for us to keep us alive, the housekeeping staff who kept every corner of the facility clean and even the patients around me trying to help each other and talk them through their struggles. There was kindness and compassion. Despite their challenges, everyone continued to give, care, and support, reminding me that even in the toughest times, there is always kindness and strength to be found.

After that night, my attitude towards life changed. I started taking life with ease, one day at a time. I started being less harsh on myself. Day by day, I started appreciating what I had. I was grateful to the people around me and their love. I was a changed woman. It took me a few months to recover completely and one year down the line, I was blessed with a baby girl.

That was you, Shah Rukh, who made me believe that even in the darkest times, there is a way to find light. Your portrayal of Aman Mathur was not just a role; it was like you were silently whispering a message to me. You gave me the hope I so desperately needed, reminding me that even when life seems too hard, there is always a way to find meaning, to keep going, and to make every moment count. You showed me that even in the face of inevitable loss, the courage to love and give is the truest form of strength. It was you who reminded me that there is always a way to rise above, and that message is what kept me going when I thought I could not.

My admiration for your strength, acceptance, and perseverance in the face of suffering grew stronger. You never let sorrow define you. Instead, you wore your pain like armour, transforming every hardship into strength, every setback into a story of resilience. And in that moment, I realized, perhaps that is why you move me so deeply. Because beyond the larger-than-life persona, beyond the silver screen, you are someone who has truly lived, loved, lost, and yet continued to shine.

Shah Rukh, I owe my life to you. Had it not been that night in the hospital watching you fighting against all odds, I might, as well, not be alive today. As you opened your arms for love and positivity in your personal life, I, too, open my heart to life's ups and downs. You taught me to live with purpose, love with all your heart, and appreciate the beauty of life despite its challenges. Shah Rukh, your presence has given me hope and brought a wave of positivity into my life that I will cherish forever.

Love You

Priyanka

Couple Goals

Dear Shah Rukh,

I love everything about you. From your acting skill to your witty replies, from your awards to the charity you do, and from those cute dimples to the eight packs you have, the list is endless. Every damn thing about you makes my heart go uummmmm... Of all these, there is one thing that stands out and I am filled with eternal respect towards you. The one thing due to which *meri nazron me apki izzat aur dil me apki mohabbat aur bhi bad jati hai* is your commitment towards your wife and family. So, this letter I want to dedicate to your better half, to the love of your life and to the woman who has had your back always.

Dear Gauri Ma'am,

I love you and I admire you a lot. I have seen you grow from a wife to a mother, from an artist to an entrepreneur. You have shown us that a woman can wear multiple hats without compromising on her dreams.

As a woman, I deeply admire you for the incredible path you have forged—not just for yourself, but as an example for countless women like me. The resilience, the strength and the boundless creativity that you portray in your work and in your life fuels us with an energy that keeps us moving towards our own aspirations. As a successful producer and a leading interior designer, your journey shows us how passion and talent, when nurtured, can bloom into something extraordinary.

Your ability to balance your professional ambitions with a fulfilling personal life is awe-inspiring. It is remarkable how you have created a home filled with love, stability, and encouragement, even while managing your career.

It is amazingly satisfying to see you and Shah Rukh Sir together. Whenever I look at you two together, my heart swells with admiration. The way you are there for each other is a benchmark for a strong marriage. In thick and thin, in sickness and health, you always stand by each other, hand in hand, shoulder to shoulder.

People say you complement and complete each other. Well, I beg to differ. If you ask me, I feel you both are already whole, individual masterpieces in your own right. But when you come together, you enhance each other's qualities. Much like adding an extra touch of charm to an already beautiful masterpiece elevating it into something extraordinary. Your relationship is a couple's goal for so many of us.

Once Charles Dickens said, *Lucky is a man who is the first love of a woman but luckiest is a woman who is the last love of a man.*

Well, Shah Rukh Sir is an absolutely fateful man, for he is the first love of so many pretty ladies out there, including me. But Ma'am, you are the only love of his life.

The thought of being exclusive, and of being someone's entire world, is a dream cherished by many, and you, Ma'am, have turned it into a beautiful reality. Your love story is a one-of-a-kind marvel, a story that stands the test of time, challenges and dizzying heights of fame.

It is so heartwarming to hear Shah Rukh Sir speak about you being his anchor, his confidante, and his source of strength. The way he adores and respects you, even after decades of togetherness, gives us a glimpse of the heartfelt bond you share.

For a woman, her husband is her pride. Her strength and confidence come from the love and respect she receives from her husband. The grace and elegance you elude every day, Ma'am, is a genuine reflection of how secure and cherished you are in your relationship. You beautifully exemplify that when a woman knows she is the centre of her husband's world, she blooms like a flower, she is fierce like a lioness, and she is unstoppable like a force of nature.

When we, the women, see Shah Rukh Sir step up for you, support your dreams and share in the joys and challenges of parenting, we look at our husbands, lying on the couch and mindlessly scrolling through their phones. We wonder, does a man like him even exist? The respect and admiration he has for you, the way he makes you feel special, loved, and secure, it is a partnership that many can only dream of. Our husbands admiring us is a farfetched thought if only they could pick up their socks by themselves!

Yes, it is love, but it is also a rare and deep understanding that elevates both of you. It is not just about grand gestures but the small acts of love and companionship that Shah Rukh Sir embodies. Seeing the way he respects and uplifts you, sets a bar so high that we cannot help but wish for even a glimpse of that in our own lives. You have shown us what true partnership looks like, and for that, we salute you both!

Every woman wants a husband like yours, Ma'am. But let us accept it, not everyone can handle the pressure of being a wife like you. It takes a lot of patience and trust to be comfortable when your husband is the 'King of Romance' (pun intended). You know, women are envious and possessive. They are insecure and if their partner is in a profession like your husband's, it is tough to give that space for him to grow. Even after twelve years of my marriage, whenever I see my husband talking to another woman, I am uncomfortable, jealous, and insecure. My eyes and mind are fixated on him as if he is being followed by *ACP Pradyumna.*

Oh yes! I am a jealous creature. I think all women are to some extent. Jealousy and possessiveness are ingrained in us, especially when it comes to our partners. The idea of seeing our husbands or boyfriends even smile at another woman, let alone share a moment of connection, feels like a tiny dagger to the heart.

And don't get us wrong, it is not about mistrust or insecurity, it is more about how deeply we love.

It is this fierce and consuming love that makes us protective, sometimes overly so. We want to believe that we are the centre of their world as they are ours. We want to be the one and only they turn to for warmth, comfort, and affection. It is our primal need, our basic instinct to guard our most precious possession.

At the same time, we know how irrational and unfair we are being to them but cannot help it. These feelings, though irrational and overdramatic, are born out of deep love. It is because our hearts are so tightly tied to theirs that the thought of sharing even a fragment with someone else feels unbearable. It is this intensity of emotion that often manifests as jealousy or possessiveness. We are not trying to control them; we are trying to hold on to what matters most to us.

But love thrives in freedom, not constraint. We learn this from you, Ma'am. The way you have given Shah Rukh Sir space to grow while remaining his pillar of support is praiseworthy. I must say, you have been very understanding and poised. Despite being aware that your husband is and will always be surrounded by gorgeous women all the time, you have carried yourself with grace and poise. Your belief in him shines through your actions.

Through all his highs and lows, you have been there for him. You have been his rock. His anchor providing stability in a life filled with chaos and challenges. I dare say he would not be the Shah Rukh Khan we all adore without your understanding, encouragement and love. Will you agree with me, Ma'am, if I say you are his ultimate support system and his lifeline?

Without your trust and confidence in him, believe me, he would have lost his sanity. I can say this because I can make my husband go nuts with the snap of a finger. And believe me, when I say this, every woman can take her husband for a spin, if she wants to, that is the power women hold. No one should test her patience.

Ma'am, you are the reason Shah Rukh Sir has reached this height. Yes, it is his talent, too, but you are his strength and the driving force behind his success. We are grateful to you, ma'am, for bestowing upon us the world-renowned and adored Shah Rukh Khan, and for being the foundation that allows him to shine so brightly. Your trust in him is a gift to us all.

Ma'am, you have inspired countless women to dream big and expect nothing less than a love that uplifts them. Together, you both redefine the meaning of true companionship.

Shah Rukh Sir always says, "I am the best". Yes, he is. But for millions of us, you both, as a couple, are *The Best*. You have a rock-solid foundation in your relationship, and I pray it grows stronger with every passing day. I look up to you both as a couple. You have been a source of inspiration for a lot of us.

With this letter, I want to take a moment to appreciate and admire both of you. Everything about you two, including your love, support, and respect for one another and how you have brought up your children, is an example to modern couples. I adore seeing you two together and I love you both. I sincerely wish that every Shah Rukh finds their Gauri.

Love You Ma'am

Priyanka

Crazy Six

Dear Shah Rukh,

You have a huge fan following all over the world and my family is no different. There are my cousin brothers, who feel over the top when I call them *Don Bhai*. My sisters are more than enthusiastic about you. Aunts and uncles always side with me when a debate, "Shah Rukh Vs XYZ" starts. We all love you very much. But today, I want to speak about those members of the family whose love for you has no boundaries, no conditions.

You remember my aunt, who introduced you to me, right? Even after thirty-two years, her eyes lighten up, she would blush, would sound dreamy and gaze into a distance while talking about you. She reminds me of the day she first spoke about you to me. Even after decades, her fondness for you reflects in her body language. She may not be assertive or too vocal about her feelings for you, but the undercurrent of a deep admiration for you reflects in her voice every time she speaks of you. She was the one who opened the door to your influence in our lives and she is the reason you became a part of our journey, our life.

Then there is my sister, Ekta. Her feelings for you are more of immense respect. She has an unshakable faith in you. She draws her inspiration from you, not only because of your achievements but also for your wisdom and kindness. Every time she witnesses you handling a challenge or interacting with people, it motivates her to be a better person and to aim higher in life. She hates to be labelled as your fan, (so do I). It is a distinct feeling she cannot describe that she has for you.

And do you remember me? I have been trying to pour my heart out to you with all these letters. By now, you would have had a little peek inside my heart. You would have had some understanding of my feelings towards you. I am sure you now know that you are the first thought of my day and the last dream of my night. My universe begins and ends with you. Every path I walk leads back to you. You are that one force that holds me from shattering, that one thrust that motivates me to soar high. You are the single most precious thing my heart has ever known.

And how could you forget Mom? Yeah, your magic worked on her like a charm. She likes you and likes you a lot now. She is not someone who would wear her heart on her sleeves and has a unique way of expressing her feelings, often masking the real essence with superficial comments. Yet, her admiration for you is undeniable and shines through her many little actions. She mostly has indirect and playful ways of communicating the affection she has for you, and it is evident in her reaction and the joy your work and your name bring to her.

We all are hopelessly in love with you, Shah Rukh. But, apart from the four of us, two more people in my family are your devoted admirers. None of them can speak clearly. None of them can do the daily chores without anyone's help. Yet, both love you from the core of their hearts.

One is the eldest member of my family, my grandmother. She is over eighty-five years of age. My Granny is a big fan of Bollywood movies. She has had great admiration for Mr. Jumping Jack, Jitendra. She was a die-hard fan. After Mr. Jitendra stopped making movies, she was kind of sad until you took over.

You are like a son to her. Whenever she hears you talk about your parents, her eyes moisten. The little tales you have told over the years about your mother and father, the hardships and the jolly moments, have warmed her heart. She frequently exclaims, "God bless everyone with a son like this!"

At this moment, she is bedridden, but despite her physical limitations, she wants to watch all your movies. She would watch every one of your interviews with me. Although she does not always understand everything you say, be it your jokes or words of wisdom, her enthusiasm drives her to seek an explanation. Whenever she would not understand a word you said or a joke you cracked, she would nag me to decipher and translate it to her. She would then laugh off, mumbling something in her *Bhojpuri* tone. I can bet, she says, "I love this boy so much".

To me, it is so heartwarming to watch her find comfort and joy in you, your work, your words, Shah Rukh. It is a challenging time for her. She often gets lonely, and her physical hardships only add to her suffering. But I have seen how deeply your presence and persona have affected her. For those are the precious moments she spends watching you, when she forgets her miseries and I can feel happiness flowing through her. It is as though you bring light into her life, even from a distance.

My Granny is not the only one awe-stuck with you. My daughter is there too. She is the youngest member of our family tree. She is two years old. When she started to understand and relate to things surrounding her, the songs from *Pathaan* became her instant favourite. Once we put on those two songs, she would listen and watch them intently, repeatedly. We could not change the channel for hours if those songs were playing.

I tried to bring variety to her song collection by introducing her to other actors and actresses, songs for children, lullabies, rhymes, and more. But She was stuck with those two. One day, while I was experimenting with various songs and poems for her, I played *Chand Tare* from *Yes Boss* on YouTube.

She observed and analyzed the song as she stood there. With a big smile on her face, she pointed a finger at you and screamed, "Mamma... Uncle," in a fumbling voice. Then she ran towards the television in excitement and began kissing the screen. It was a sight to see.

I was both amazed and happy, all at the same time. My heart was overflowing with emotions of love and joy. I then showed her your songs from some other movies and in each of them she recognized you and gave flying kisses. She would address you as *'Pyare Uncle'*. She loves you, Shah Rukh. I think she got this in inheritance. I am on cloud nine when someone says, *Like Mother Like Daughter*, about our liking for you.

It is your magic Shah Rukh, that a two-year-old who understands nothing recognizes you and would cheer up listening and watching you. An eighty-five-year-old would love you like her own child. Though I do not feel much difference in the way my grandma and my daughter talk about you, both clumsy and unclear, certainly the love for you shines. What is your secret? Have you ever wondered; how six ladies across four generations in the same family love you insanely in their unique ways?

It is rare, Shah Rukh, for someone to transcend generations and connect so deeply with people of all ages, but you have done it effortlessly. You have been an integral and enduring part of our lives, becoming more than just an actor, a shared thread of joy, inspiration, and love. From my daughter's innocent giggles to my grandmother's nostalgic affection, you have created a bond that unites us all. Whatever your secret may be, it is an obvious proof of the way you touch hearts, not just through your movies, but through the person you are. And for that, we will always hold you close.

Love You

Priyanka

A message from Ekta

Dear Shah Rukh,

When I told my kiddo sister, Ekta, about the letters I am writing to you, she was excited. She asked me if I could include one of her messages for you. I was more than happy to include her in my journey to reach out to you. This one is from her.

Dear Shah Rukh Sir,

I am Ekta, a 27-year-old individual whose cinematic journey began with the mesmerizing tale of *Mohabbatein.* Since that moment, your films have held a special place in my heart. Your ability to convey emotions through tears, smiles, expressions, and actions has shaped my understanding of love and relationships. While I enjoy a variety of movies, I find myself constantly drawn to stories like *Kal Ho Naa Ho, Veer-Zaara, Dear Zindagi, and Swades.* It is not just the storyline that captivates me, but your portrayal of the characters. Your passion for your craft shines through in every role, leaving me spellbound each time.

I will never forget the day I had the opportunity to see you, in person, at Hansraj College during my graduation from Delhi University. Amidst the uproar of excited fans, I stood in awe, tears streaming down my face as I realized I was witnessing you in the flesh. It is hard to articulate the emotions I felt in that moment—a mixture of disbelief, gratitude, and immense respect. While I hesitate to label myself as a "fan", there is an undeniable reverence I hold for your work, your dedication, and your humility. Your down-to-earth nature is perhaps your most endearing quality, reminding me to stay grounded even amidst success.

You have been more than just a celebrity to me; you have been a source of inspiration. Your resilience, your commitment to your family, and your unwavering work ethic have motivated me to dream big and strive for excellence. You have taught me the importance of never forgetting one's roots, no matter how high we soar in life.

As I conclude this letter, I want to express my heartfelt wishes for continued success, happiness, and good health for you and your loved ones. Your presence in the world has made it a brighter, more hopeful place, and for that, I am truly grateful.

With love and admiration,

Ekta

Seeking The Shah Rukh Khan

Dear Shah Rukh,

When people ask me why I am so deeply in love with you, I find myself at a loss for words. Sometimes, it feels like there are a hundred reasons, each more beautiful than the other, and other times, it feels like there is no reason at all, just a love so intense that it defies explanation. You cannot reason in love.

My friends annoy me by saying all sorts of absurd things about you anyone can possibly think. They will make fun of your movies, your age and looks and everything related to you to get on my nerves. Their actions are deliberately targeted towards me, provoking me to say or do something they can make fun of forever. What else are friends for?

Then there are my siblings. At any family gathering, all my cousins would gang up against me for my inclination towards you. For them, the best part of the event is to put me on the spot and make fun of you, infuriating me. But the most common questions I am always bombarded with are "Why do you love him so much?", "What is so attractive about him?"

I have tried hard to find an answer to this question, Shah Rukh, but never succeeded. My affection for you started like a little seedling that sprouted and grew into an enormous tree, holding my heart together. Now the roots are so strong that if the tree is uprooted, the entire foundation of my being would crumble.

There are nights I have slept over these thoughts; why do I feel such a strong connection to you? Is it your work or your looks? Is it your humility? Why is it that, no matter what state of mind I am in—depressed, tired, anxious, excited—your name is enough to bring a smile to my face?

I try to reason with myself why I keep falling for you every day and which aspect of your life has the most influence on me. Yes, your work is admirable. It reflects the hard work you put into it. Your characters show how passionate you are about your work. You bring your stories to life, and they live in our hearts forever. But is this reason enough to hold someone in such high regard?

Then your looks! You have proved that age is just a number. I mean that eight-packs I saw recently, the enthusiasm with which you grooved on the dance numbers, it is as if time has only added more charm and energy to you. But again, this cannot be the reason I am so hooked on you. My affection goes far beyond what meets the eye.

I then thought it must be your aura that drew me closer to you. Your humbleness and kindness. Your chivalry and the way you carry yourself with such charm and dignity. It is the warmth in your words, the sincerity in your actions, and the way you make everyone feel seen and valued. But won't you agree with me, Shah Rukh, perceiving someone's charisma solely through their work and snippets from the media, can only offer a glimpse, it can never truly capture the complete essence of who they are.

Finally, my thoughts boil down to the probability of something being wrong with me psychologically. Why else would I find someone I have only met in my dreams so irresistible and unforgettable? OR maybe we have some connection from the past life. Which one makes more sense to you, Shah Rukh? Me being psycho, right? Well, everyone says so, but I prefer to believe otherwise. I want to believe we have some heavenly connections.

In all my letters, I have spoken a lot about how you have affected my life. How you have been an epitome of love and a symbol of resilience for me. How you have inspired me and been my strength. I have spoken everything about myself.

Today, I want to know more about you. I have this strong desire to know you beyond your celebrity status. As a film star, everyone knows you. I want to know you as a person. There should be something in common between you and me.

Help me understand Shah Rukh, how you are similar or different from the people I know. What would it be like, had you been a guy from my neighborhood, a classmate in college, or a colleague at the workplace? Would you not still be you? What if we were friends? Would the love and respect I hold for you change in any way? I wish I could know "The Shah Rukh Khan", without all his fame and popularity someday. Maybe, in this quest, I will find an answer to "Why I love you".

I sometime wonder what an offscreen Shah Rukh would look like. I want to explore the factors that bring you joy and the things that ignite your anger. There must be a unique way how you process pain and sorrow—sometimes in quiet reflection, other times indulging in something else to divert your mind. For me, it is mostly screaming and throwing things around. Then there are your motivations and inspirations and the forces that keep you moving.

A family man like you must have his unique style to make his wife and children feel cherished. I often find myself pondering over thoughts like, do you go that extra mile to surprise your family and friends or are surprises a distant thought for you? Probably you may prefer a more planned way of doing things.

I want to know about your likes and dislikes in terms of, maybe food, desserts or maybe the vacation spot. I wonder if it is the hills that appeal to you more or the beaches where you would prefer to spend some quiet time. There must be some priceless possessions you own, and I am not talking about any materialistic things, a memory that you hold dear or a tiny little something that brings a beautiful smile to your face.

Will you help me know Shah Rukh, a little something about your childhood? Your favourite pranks, a pretty teacher you had your first crush on or the most notorious kid you hated secretly. There must be a cute excuse for all your pranks that always worked on your mother, a favourite actor you always imitated.

I cannot help but wonder if you were flirtatious during your college. Were you not that one boy in the college, whose contagious smile and charm spread across the campus, drawing admiration and attention wherever you went? Perhaps you were the life of every gathering, the one whose presence lit up the room and left a lasting impression on everyone you met, just as you are today.

Alright, tell me this, what is that one quality I should have to be friends with you? I would like to know what kind of company you keep and if there are any specific traits in people you avoid. As with everyone else, there has to be something you love in people and something that is absolutely intolerable. Or is it you don't have a specific preference and simply go with the flow, connecting with people as they come? I would like to understand what draws you to someone as a friend and what might make you distance yourself.

An inquisitive me always wants to know if you ever get the time to, or do you even like to reflect on your greatest fear? Like in your films, there must be moments of vulnerability you might have gone through in your life and your way of coping with them. Then there must be some dreams and fantasies, not yet materialized, that you so badly want to come to life.

I speculate that your heart overflows with strong emotions when you see those little kids on signals begging for alms and you feel strongly about the underprivileged. Then there would have been instances where watching the news, you told your wife, " These reporters will never change". Over lunch with friends, you might have expressed your frustration or concern about the state of things happening in the country.

My apologies, Shah Rukh, if my speculations and inquisitiveness felt like a third-degree to you. It is just that there are so many things, yet so little, I want to know about you. While you have shared glimpses of yourself in interviews, I am sure there is a side of you that is personal, something only your close ones truly know. I am interested in discovering that more intimate side.

If I had a superpower for a day, I would choose to be invisible and be by your side, not to intrude, but to quietly observe and understand you better. It would mean a lot to learn about the person beyond the celebrity Shah Rukh Khan.

Shah Rukh, I find myself longing to understand you better, to figure out why you hold such a special place in my heart that no one else can take. These are some of my most cherished dreams, the deep longing to connect with the real you, to know you just a little more than I do now. I truly believe in the power of dreams, and I hope that one day this one will come true. Until then, I will hold on to these dreams with hope in my heart and a sense of wonder in my eyes.

Love you,

Priyanka

Some Upon the Future Day

Dear Shah Rukh,

You know I have been longing to see you all my life. I know it is difficult, but a part of me believes it is not impossible. A part of me thinks it will happen, some upon the future day. That phrase has stayed with me, so much so that I poured my feelings into a poem I wrote in 10th grade titled 'Some Upon the Future Day.'

This poem is a whisper of my soul, a reflection of my hopes and dreams. I wanted to share it with you because it carries everything I have wanted to say but never found the words for. I hope it resonates with you as deeply as it does with me.

Some Upon A Future Day

Some upon a future day

When what is now is not
When all the faults and follies are forgot
We will meet
Upon some future day

Some upon a future day
When the sun will shine bright
And bless us with its pleasant light
We will meet
Upon some future day

Some upon a future day
When the flowers will bloom
Their fragrance will make our hearts swoon
We will meet
Upon some future day

Some upon a future day
When spring will come soon
The birds will sing a melodious tune
We will meet
Upon some future day

Some upon a future day
When bright the moon will shine
I will be yours, you will be mine
We will meet
Upon some future day

Some upon a future day
When this dream will come true
And I will be forever with you
We will meet
Upon THAT future day❤

Love You,

Priyanka

Love You Hamesha

Dear Shah Rukh,

In my first letter, I spoke about how some whimsical dreams urging me to reach out to you. Well, I lied. It was not some fancy dream because of which I would pick up my pen and pour my heart out to you. I am not that insane. I am more than that!

It was an overwhelming force within me, the one I could not silence, one that demanded to be heard, one that whispered your name in moments of joy, sorrow, and everything in between. And so, I wrote, not because I chose to, but because I had no other choice.

My quest to reach you began way back in my twenties. I was enthusiastic and ambitious. The reason I chose Mumbai as my first job location was a firm belief that I would meet you there. I did whatever a twenty-something-year-old can do to meet the love of her life.

Then life happened, and priorities changed. And as with most of us, our most cherished dreams often take a back seat, making way for a career, marriage and family. During those days I was trying hard to achieve an equilibrium between personal and professional commitments, I often found myself juggling the demands of a budding career and the responsibilities of my newly formed family. There were peak frustrating days and most depressing nights. But my desire to connect to you never died.

You know Shah Rukh, even after the fire had died, a little spark remains. And all it takes is a little breeze to ignite it again. My pursuit to find you is like that. Buried deep within me, it never extinguished and kept my heart warm. All it took was a thought, a weird dream and your name to bring them alive again.

I know it is difficult to reach you. So many people want to meet you every day. Some will write hundreds of tweets to gain your attention, others will spend days and months outside Mannat to get a hug from you. I understand, that even if you like it, it is not possible to meet everyone in this lifetime, Shah Rukh.

Though I salute their zeal and emotions and am absolutely envious of them for having met you, touched you, or having gotten your response, I do not want you to know me as a random fan. A phone call, a handshake, a selfie or a hug, is not what I am seeking. And even though I would love to be part of a crowd screaming your name when they see you in person, a glimpse of you is not what I am looking for. I am seeking to know the person I have admired throughout my life, a little beyond his public persona. I am seeking to be known by the person who has the deepest impact on my life.

When the idea of writing you a letter struck me, I thought I would write a simple letter and post it to your office or home address. How naïve I was! I wrote a few of them, but as simple as it sounded; I realized that not only the letters may get lost but also all I want to say cannot be captured in a few letters. Then I thought I would write to you on certain occasions, like a festival, your movie release or on your birthday. I immediately realized you would get millions and trillions of messages during those periods. My message may never get across.

Disheartened by my thoughts, I almost gave up the idea of posting those letters to you, but I did not stop writing them. When I had a few of them, I read them over and over again, visualizing what it would be like you reading one of those on a cozy afternoon sipping on your coffee. The image of you reading one of my messages gave me a thrill that I have not experienced in what felt like a lifetime. I started compiling those letters on my laptop, and that is how this book started.

Every letter has been a nostalgic experience. With each letter, I have re-lived a phase of my life with you. All those beautiful memories that faded with time resurfaced, giving me eternal happiness. In the process, I have reconnected with so many people I had lost touch with. It transported me back in time, where I saw the little me talking to the dolls about you, the teenage me asserting myself to be heard. I saw my twenty-five-year-old self roaming on the streets of Mumbai as a free bird and I witnessed a devastated me rekindling hope in life.

There were moments of vulnerability and immense connection. There were times when I was filled with gratitude, and then there were instances of longing and quiet reflection. I laughed, and I cried while scribbling these letters. In each of these notes, I have tried to draw a picture of my heart, a fragment of my mind. It has been an emotionally overwhelming journey, and it is extremely difficult for me to pen down this last letter.

I have so much more to say. A few pages cannot be enough to pour out my heart and soul. Through this series of letters, I have tried communicating my feelings to you. The feelings of love, admiration, and gratitude that go beyond the boundaries of words. Shah Rukh, how can a few words describe what I feel for you? Those feelings cannot be contained in some humble words.

You have been with me ever since my childhood and to my youth and till today. You, Shah Rukh, are the only constant in my ever-changing life. Your life is an inspiration for hundreds of millions of people, me being one of them. Your hard work is reflected in your movies, your sense of humour makes me roll on the floor with laughter, and the thoughts you share in your interviews leave a deep impact on me. Yet, your humility is something I love the most.

You have taught me so much. “I am the best”, “I run my own race”, “The only way to succeed is to work hard”, “To love a woman is to respect her”, “First be rich and then be a philosopher”, are some remarks you have made in your interviews and my admiration for you deepened, while my love for you blossomed in my heart with every passing day. These thoughts shaped my life. I incorporate them into my life.

You have been my childhood love and high school sweetheart in the small town of Varanasi. In the hectic life of Mumbai, you were my stress buster, my happy hormones. You were my only companion on the lonely nights of Chennai. In all my highs and lows, you have been a constant presence, an enduring influence.

Your actions and words have provided me comfort in challenging times and company when I have been alone. When life threw the most difficult challenges at me, your fortitude served as a beacon of hope. In moments of joy, your infectious laughter echoed, and in moments of sorrow, your words provided me courage and comfort.

Through every letter, I have laid bare the essence of my journey. As I reflect on the pages turned, I want to extend my deepest gratitude for being the unwavering force that guided me through life's maze. From being a submissive girl to finding my voice, from asking others for help to doing it myself and from giving up on life to taking one day at a time, I owe my life to you, Shah Rukh.

You have taught me the art of self-acceptance and resilience. You made me believe in focusing on myself and there is no competition greater than competing with yourself. Thank You Shah Rukh. Thank You for being there. Just knowing you exist makes all the difference.

Throughout the book, I have expressed my deep admiration and intense love for you, often failing to find the right words for it. However, this book is not just about defining what I feel for you; it is also about letting you know that in this crazy journey of life, you were always a part of it, making everything just a little better. I love you, Shah Rukh, not because of who you are, but because of who I am when I think of you.

As this book concludes, I find myself drowned, yet again, in your love. Re-living the old chapters of my life, I now know love has no reason, no age, and no language. It is just love. It is YOU. For me, you, Shah Rukh Khan is the synonym for true love. From the wallpaper of my cell phone to the walls of my heart, you and your love surround me everywhere.

Love You Hamesha

Priyanka